LIFESPACE

LIFESPACE

DESIGNS
FOR TODAY'S
LIVING

SPIROS ZAKAS WITH MARGARET MINER

MACMILLAN PUBLISHING CO., INC.

NEW YORK

PHOTOGRAPHY BY
ARMAN AGRESTI AND
PETER ZAKAS

Macmillan Publishing Co., Inc.
866 Third Avenue, New York, N.Y. 10022
Collier Macmillan Canada, Ltd.

Library of Congress Cataloging in Publication Data

Zakas, Spiros.
　　Lifespace.

　　　1.　Interior decoration.　2.　Space (Architecture)
I.　Miner, Margaret, joint author.　II.　Title.
NK2115.Z34　　　747　　　77–24208
ISBN: 0-02-633410-0

First Printing 1977

Printed in the United States of America

CONTENTS

DEDICATION

There comes a time   I am happy
when everyone   that I was fortunate
sits around   to have been
and thinks   helped
of his beginnings   by so many

From a course
in antiques
Stella Zakas
struck a chord
Peter Maduros
struck a few more
Thank you

LIFESPACE

I am a home designer. I also do many other kinds of design work, from pieces of furniture to offices, restaurants, and hotels. But home design is the most demanding, challenging, and satisfying. In a home, the interaction between a person and the environment is intense, intimate, and varied. And a home mirrors those who live there.

In my work I see the same mistakes in homes over and over again, and when I say "mistake," I don't mean something that I don't like personally, I mean something that's wrong and annoying for the person who has to live with it. In talking about these problems with a client, I sometimes find that at first we seem almost to be talking about different subjects; it takes a while before we're in key with each other. Part of my job is showing people new ways of looking at their homes, new approaches to the problems. Successful design depends to a surprising extent on attitudes and ideas. Without certain basic concepts, without being tuned into and aware of certain aspects of space and architecture, it's almost impossible to create a pleasing environment. You have to be conscious of yourself. You have to observe yourself and the pattern of your life at home. You're the one your home is for.

Most mistakes in design come from worrying about the wrong things. When I'm told a long story about what colors are going into the guest room, and what fabric is going to be used for the living room drapes, and how much carpet is going to be spread around, I know the results will be poor. And I can't really help. I can't, for example, suggest another material for drapes, when I have no idea whether drapes are needed at all. And one of the first things people always want to talk about is color, which is usually the last thing I think about. To me color is like the patina on a bronze sculpture. It *is* important; it does enhance the beauty of the piece. But it's also a superficial factor, incidental to the underlying structure. With the cosmetic approach to decorating, the first thing you think about is color, and you aim at creating pretty surfaces. The prettiness, though, may not relate to the lives that are going on in the home.

I've had people talk to me for a half hour about how they're redoing their homes without ever describing the character of the architecture, the organization of the space, or the quality of the light. Moreover, they never explain how they'd like to use the space. We all have individual styles of living that should be reflected in the design of our homes. There isn't any "right" design or any formula for living. Each home must be planned uniquely.

Designing your home is one activity in which you should be self-centered. I don't mean selfish in the sense of running out and making all kinds of extravagant purchases. I mean reshaping your home so that it has more of what you enjoy and less of what you dislike. I mean planning to make it possible for you to do more of what you like to do, planning to be comfortable and free. The way to do it can't be found in a department store catalog or a magazine article. The way comes from your consciousness of yourself and your environment.

It's very common to feel insecure about your decorating ideas and to want reassurance. But if you keep adjusting your plans so that they're more like what your neighbor did or Jackie Onassis or someone else did, you'll end up with miscellaneous secondhand ideas. Ultimately, you're the authority of what you like and need around you. It's your personality that pulls it altogether.

There's no need to force "creative" touches. I'm reminded of "creative" projects kids used to get in school, and still do: cutting out hearts and lace for Valentine's Day, making potholders, coloring in pictures. A lot of creative decorating projects are about the same.

To have a home that's creative, interesting, charming, you don't have to be artistic or eccentric; you don't have to live in a cottage or an apartment in the Dakota. You have to design for your own original self. You probably have to clear out of your head a big collection of conventions and status symbols. And you have to start really seeing and feeling your surroundings.

There are lots of dream books on home design, full of pictures of rooms you'll never live in. I meet people who have drawers full of glossy magazine articles and never get around to repainting the den. And I think the "home" that received the most publicity recently was the vice-president's house decorated by the Nelson Rockefellers, which was never lived in at all.

It's good to have dreams, but it's depressing if they're so far from reality that you can't even get started.

Sometimes you can get started on a dream but you can't follow through. I have some friends who started furnishing their living room about twelve years ago with a fine camelback sofa. Unfortunately, the reality is that they can't afford to do the whole room this way. And they won't go with anything less. So today the room still lacks adequate seating, lighting, interest, and, of course, use.

I have other friends who carry around swatches and color charts for years and spend more money on subscriptions to decorating magazines than on actual renovation. In the meantime they're embarrassed to have people in. There are lots of good excuses for putting off making changes—you'll be moving in a few years, the children are at the destructive age, you're waiting to win the lottery. But someday in the future you'll start living the way you want to—you hope.

I love the present. This book is about what you can do today. It's meant to get you started. It gives ideas on how and where to begin, what concepts to keep in mind, what clichés to throw out.

It might be nice to live in a dream house or a palace, but not many of us do. We live in homes that aren't ideal, that are, to say the least, a challenge. But that's true of many elegant homes, as well. They didn't start out in perfect shape. Of course, it's more fun to think about the things we want than to do something about the things we need. I know it's the wants that make life worth living, and next to them the needs are boring. But I feel it's a good idea to take care of the needs first to some degree. When it's done you feel freer.

A small budget shouldn't hold you back. You can begin with a plan, a few hundred dollars, and an appreciation of what's important.

A few months ago I visited a new home that the owners were extremely proud of. There was a Plexiglas staircase leading from the foyer to the dining room. The staircase was incredibly expensive. But the dining room chairs were dinky and uncomfortable. The money had been put in the wrong place. First be sure your guests can sit through a

11

meal comfortably. Then worry about spectacular effects.

Without a single antique or status symbol, you can have a home that's unique, refreshing, personal, and comfortable. You do need seating that's kind to the rear end. You don't need a palace. In fact most palaces are dark and drafty, as well as hard to heat, cool, maintain, clean, and decorate.

As for dream homes, I've been in a few, and they have problems of their own. They tend to be exaggerated and moody and hard to relax in. They're good to study, because you can learn from them. But in the end you'll learn most by doing.

The character of your home affects the quality of your life, your feelings about yourself, and other people's feelings about you.

When a child writes down where he lives, it may look something like this:

Tommy Smith
25 Berry Avenue
Mamaroneck, N.Y.
The Solar System
Universe

It's a joke, but based on deep feelings. Your home is *your* place in the universe. Feelings of home radiate outward from the heart of the home (the private and family spaces—bedroom, kitchen, den) into the neighborhood and perhaps much farther beyond—to your *home*land.

When a client comes to me not satisfied with his home, I begin by asking if he feels at home in his neighborhood. Sometimes people stay in a bad situation out of inertia or sentimentality when they could move. Certainly, before any major work is started, I try to be sure the clients are reasonably happy where they are. Of course, some people are hard to figure. I was presenting plans to one Long Island couple, who seemed proud of their house and kept insisting I get the job finished in July. When I asked, "Why the rush?" they said they needed the house ready in July because they were moving in September. I threw out my plans and started to work on the new house.

One good result of the hard economic times we've had lately, especially in cities, is that more people are moving into nonresidential or run-down neighborhoods, trying to claim and reclaim new spaces for living. Brownstones are being renovated and lofts converted. People are moving into warehouses, churches, and railway stations. In Chicago, I see blocks and blocks of overcrowded, poor housing and then blocks and blocks of semiabandoned factories and warehouses. It can't be long before people start moving into these spaces. I have two friends who've bought a bank in New Jersey that's been empty since the Depression. I, myself, live in a building that was built in 1890 on the waterfront in New York City as a carpenter's home, shop, and warehouse. Not only are the economics of the situation good, but there's a strong satisfaction in becoming part of a neighborhood that was almost destroyed by changing times—and banks, realtors, etc. New people are returning and trying to save the old buildings. We have a chance.

The success of various types of alternate housing points up the fact that a home can be created even when the conditions aren't ideal. The quality of a home depends most on the spirit and vision that goes into it. Some of the loveliest, most exciting homes I've seen are in dilapidated industrial buildings and old, unpromising farmhouses. Once you step inside your home and close your door, you're in your own territory. You can do what you want, in any style you want. Outside there are endless rules you have to follow. At home you make your own rules.

Your home should be a refuge and a place of refreshment. In the 1960s the role of personal space and inner life was downgraded. Life was restless. Apartments were crash pads.

I love action and movement and travel. I work all over the world. But everyone needs a base. A place to revive, not just crash. A place to be with friends. A place of solitude. A place for lovers. A place for family.

People who want their homes to be attractive sometimes make them into showcases for objects. But a home is first of all for living, and it should express the feelings and attitudes of those who live there.

Unfortunately, too many homes aren't anything like this at all. They're impersonal and exactly like a million other homes, though the owners want exactly the opposite.

What goes wrong? The main problem I think, is, that we're bombarded with so many commercial images and old-fashioned ideas of what a home's supposed to be like. The most difficult stage in designing a home is the very beginning. It's in developing a new approach, looking honestly at your life and environment, realizing that there isn't a ready-made plan or style that can be fitted to your life. When you buy an instant "look," you end up making your life

fit the style. When I work with clients I try to find out about their lives, not their ideas about style. I want to know how a family moves in a home and what they'd like to do there that they can't. I discuss many possibilities. I urge clients to get involved personally.

In this book I want to do the same thing I do working directly with a client: Make you aware of possibilities, get you involved in design.

I understand very well the anxieties people feel trying something new. After all, when you walk into someone's home for the first time, you see that person in a new light. I'm sure anyone reading this book can go through a home without knowing the owners and tell a great deal about them. There's nothing more revealing than a home, and it's sometimes intimidating to think other people are sizing you up the same way you would them.

I also know it isn't easy to find well-made, imaginative furnishings. In fact this is one reason I do furniture and lighting design. And this experience taught me that often you can make individually designed furnishings more easily and cheaply than you can buy them. You can also take the same ideas and develop more complicated and extravagant designs, which can be fascinating and fun but not necessarily better.

This realization was a long step for someone like me, who grew up in the antique business and likes luxury. But the more sophisticated concept of luxury is oriented toward a person's *experiences* (sensations and emotions) in a space rather than toward the *things* that are put into it.

13

GOOD TASTE

Everyone thinks he has good taste. In a discussion of bad taste present company is always excepted. Of course, people secretly worry about their taste. That's why they read fashion magazines and decorators' columns. The trouble is you have to have good taste to evaluate the advice you get.

Fortunately, taste can be learned—by exposure to beautiful places and things. One proof that taste is acquired through experience is that a person may have perfect taste in one culture and make blunders in another. You may be able to pick a chic evening coat for the opera, but could you pick an appropriate kimono for the Kabuki?

The brain is constantly and almost unconsciously picking up bits of information. Most people aren't aware of learning rules of good taste, so they say its a "feeling"—that white socks don't go with a Brooks Brothers suit, that Carmen Miranda translucent wedgies aren't the thing when applying for a job at the Frick Museum.

The first step in acquiring good taste is becoming sensitive to a web of cultural associations. The second step is freeing yourself from the web.

Americans have no single tradition that is a touchstone for excellence in home design. Most of the so-called traditional furniture you see in department stores is an inaccurate imitation of European styles. Nor have different ethnic groups consistently carried over the traditions of the countries they came from. My family, for instance, is Greek and now lives in Florida. Since the climate of Florida resembles that of Greece, you might think the Greeks there would have adapted some of the traditional features of Greek homes to their American life, such as stone floors, high ceilings, or balconies outside bedroom windows.

Instead they've adjusted to the society they live in. This is fine in a way, but because of the national scope of manufacturing and marketing, homes in Florida aren't much different from homes in Minnesota, Oregon, or Arizona. The same furniture that's available in one place is generally available across the nation. Fabrics may tend to be lighter weight and there may be more aluminum furniture, but the styling and mood, or feeling, is the same.

There's an American "look" in home design, but it hasn't evolved over time in response to the needs of American households. Instead it's a status-oriented, almost arbitrary image, rapidly popularized in mass-media advertising, movies, and TV shows. It's up for grabs which variation of pseudotraditional furnishings will be next year's success. Instead of responding to the freedom that a multicultural, multi-ethnic society could allow, we tend to latch onto makeshift images: the homey image, the swinger image, the young married image. The styles created for those images are largely in poor taste—not because they're gross, but because there's no purpose or sense to them. Taste can be whimsical but not inane.

Because of the mass-media exploitation of images, I usually advise clients who want to learn more about design and style not to read the popular women's magazines and home beautification magazines, particularly when they're looking for ideas. Many times they end up with gimmicks instead. Once you know what you want, the magazines can be helpful in teaching the how-to's of managing it.

To develop a sense of good design spend more time at museums, with art books, and with the more serious design magazines, such as *Domus* (an Italian publication), *Interiors*, *Interior Design*, *Progressive Architecture*, *Architectural Digest*, and so on. Get to know the best that there is and was; in every period there have been progressive innovations in design that represent a better way to live. Get the feeling of different materials, colors, and lighting, of the flow of line in a piece of furniture, of different spatial proportions. Don't limit yourself to looking at lamps and chairs and your neighbors' houses. Look at paintings and sculpture and chateaux. Even if what you see is far beyond what you ever thought of or could afford for yourself, your experience can be reflected in your home. Even nonvisual arts can contribute by affecting the kind of person you are and the emotions you project into the space around you.

Travel should be one of the best ways to extend your experience and understanding. I have some friends who particularly enjoy traveling to countries very different from ours. In their home they have old maps from India, weapons from Rumania, embroidered silks from China, and porcelain from Japan. But when I travel, so often I see tourists buying, buying, buying at the souvenir stands in front of churches and museums. Such a waste of money. I wonder why they don't search out the unusual.

Visit as many different and different kinds of homes as possible. Color photos of nice, neat rooms are no substitute for stepping into the space of a home and getting the sense of living there. And don't be afraid of asking questions; most people are pleased that guests are interested in why a certain arrangement was made, how it has worked, and so forth.

Finally, keep your eyes open wherever you are, on the beach, in a bar, at the theater, in the park. New ideas for using colors, shapes, lights, materials develop from your total experience.

Good taste comes from curiosity, observation, and experience with good things. The more you see, the more you understand what's going on around you and within you, the more discriminating you become.

I've heard a thousand times, "Oh you can't define good taste or good design in a home," but it's not all that mysterious.

A home is in good taste when it is clearly and uniquely the home of those who live there and when being in it imparts pleasing and comfortable feelings.

This intimate relationship between a person and a home can't be faked. A wall full of eighteenth-century hunting prints doesn't warm up a library if the library belongs to someone who never rode a horse, much less chased a fox, and who just sent his secretary to Saks to pick up something for the wall. There are all kinds of little giveaways. There'll be no continuity of interest and attitude between the prints and anything else in the house; with this approach to décor, everything in the home is apt to be unrelated and disjointed. The prints probably won't be hung to the best advantage. There may be no rationale to the sequence in which they're hung. And so forth. If the man had instead put up something that interested him, perhaps something connected with his work, he'd understand how it should be presented.

A well-designed home fulfills the functions of a

Good taste reflects a personality and way of life. It may be formal or casual, spare or lush, serious or humorous. In the first photo, the Queen Ann chairs set a formal and traditional mood for dining. My own dining area, shown next, is intimate and comfortable. People sit around the table for hours. The third eating area is an extension of the patio, simple and easy to wash down. The esthetic focus is on the view. The last photo shows another counter with banquettes, but the mood is camp, not country. The design is particularly suited to homes with limited space.

home and isn't just decorated space. Your home should work for you. It's a place for activity and rest, not a pretty thing to be gazed at.

A tasteful home isn't full of imitations and clichés; it isn't boring. Ideally, it's intriguing, surprising, clever, imaginative, fresh. The wider your general experience and the more thought you give each decision, the more chance you can avoid banalities. But this means rethinking the standards of your immediate society, of your friends and neighbors. Mostly what people believe to be tasteful depends too much on what group they belong to. Some groups are into tradition, others insist on contemporary styles, some follow the magazines. It's difficult to evolve a personal, individual approach while reading the same publications and shopping at the same stores as everyone else you know. Tired sources deliver

tired ideas. Your own interests and needs are your best resource.

Many clichés are the result of pretentiousness. There's something charming about walking into a young couple's apartment that's unfinished, with pillows on the floor and books stacked in the corners. That's as far as they've gotten. It's not so charming when they've gone out and arranged a bank loan to buy a living room set so they'll look as though they have it all together. The first says "adjusting," the second says "pretending."

To be attractive a home does need good furnishings, but not necessarily the best or most expensive. But the simplest, most basic rule is to pick honest furnishings that don't attempt to be or do more than is necessary or possible. Like any good rule, it has exceptions, but it won't lead you wrong.

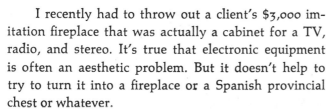

I recently had to throw out a client's $3,000 imitation fireplace that was actually a cabinet for a TV, radio, and stereo. It's true that electronic equipment is often an aesthetic problem. But it doesn't help to try to turn it into a fireplace or a Spanish provincial chest or whatever.

If you do have an excellent piece of furniture or art that you love, or even a plant, then this can be used to set the tone of a space, and everything else can be keyed to it. I'm reminded of the Japanese tea ceremony, which takes place in a separate very simple room and is centered on one beautiful object. The idea isn't to adore the object but to compose the mind.

For a space to be well designed and pleasing, nothing extraordinarily expensive or fine is needed. The relationship among the elements is what counts.

I believe that in every home there should be some unusual, beautiful color, although someone with very severe taste might disagree with this criterion. If you can afford only modest, plain furniture, and the architecture of your space is nothing to boast about, then color can become especially important: not great expanses of color, which most likely will just emphasize the problems, but one or two rays, so to speak, of delightful colors that please you.

Finally, a good home must be clean. It can be messy and disordered, and the fabrics can be rather worn; but dust, stains, grime, and grit are depressing. In a city, particularly, it can be hard to keep a place clean, but usually more use of modern materials will help. When I see busy people coping with waxed floors, upholstered furniture, silk lampshades, velvet drapes, and so on, I sometimes feel that instead of

19

Plants change the tone of a space.

21

living in their homes they're chained by them. If cleaning is a problem, plan so you can simplify it.

Don't follow strict rules of taste to the point of boredom. I can't think of any rule that might not be broken with good results. For example, mixing strong, contrasting colors like red and black is usually considered too loud, but with the right balance of color and in an appropriate space it can be striking and pleasing. Or you might break a rule by working against the character of an interior instead of with it. Thus, I suggested to one client setting a row of small Christmas lights in the ceiling molding of her traditional, classically proportioned living room. The contrast created an exciting freshness the room needed.

Good taste is a conservative concept. It implies restraint and quietness, and rules out vulgarity and conspicuous extravagance. And it's true that in a home, which is to some degree a semipublic space, restraint is a virtue. It's comfortable and puts others at ease. But sometimes it's a banal virtue. It's the same with clothes: as much as I admire the timeless grace of a Chanel suit, sometimes I like women dressed like Cher.

Great art, humor, passion, fantasy—all break through the restraints of good taste and shouldn't be excluded from any home where they're wanted. There's even a place for vulgarity. A neon sign with your name on it isn't exactly tasteful, perhaps, but are you ever going to see your name in lights if you don't put it there yourself? Maybe it would be pushy to put the sign out on the front porch, but in a bedroom, why not?

Don't be oppressed by stuffy, uptight standards. Too many people are living in tense competitive worlds with all kinds of rules about what you buy, who you're seen with, what image you project. The Gucci-Pucci world of status symbols is full of people who can't even have fun unless they're doing the in thing. Couples who ten years ago skied and served Scotch now play tennis and take cocaine.

A houseful of status products doesn't make it. Each item may be attractive enough; the Barcelona chairs, Argo lamps, Steinway piano, Oriental rugs, etc. But they've all been seen again and again. Sometimes the entire setup of the apartment is predictable from one look through the door. The brand names make the owners feel secure, but the effect is stale.

In the world of antiques, the rule is that if it's authentic it's in good taste. Antiquers put together rooms that would be interesting or even charming in a museum. But in real life they're precious, uncomfortable, and a little scary. The people who live there haven't exposed themselves at all. The home might have been created for ghosts.

And then there's the world of pseudotraditional middle America where the homes look like TV stages. I feel intimidated in these rooms, under pressure to act like someone in a TV drama, very nice and ordinary. I think other people subconsciously feel this way, too, and hide deeper or more interesting feelings and thoughts.

Well-balanced people don't live in small worlds or even a small span of time. Their ideas include the past, the present, and even anticipations of the future. They aren't afraid to let themselves be seen and felt, and in a home it's all-important to feel the presence of people. Good taste goes beyond aesthetics, for it also means creating an environment in which you and your guests can be relaxed and in communication, not tense, controlled, and artificial.

SPACE AND THE FUNCTIONS OF A HOME

Your home is a shelter, not just from the weather but from all the world outside. Your home shouldn't add to your worries and your burdens. But too often in planning a home people neglect (of all things!) their own comfort and interests. They arrange their homes according to standardized, even ritualized patterns, and in the end they don't really enjoy the home. It becomes just one more thing to be taken care of instead of something you enjoy.

There are many designers who love a client who goes on vacation while they go to work. This is the one kind of client I can't cope with. I don't feel that I'm doing my job by designing a "model" home. Are "model" people going to live in it?

To do my job, I need to ask questions and observe how a home is used day to day by those who live there, to see what works well and what doesn't work at all. As changes are actually made, I want to be certain the plan is as practical in real life as it seemed on paper—if it isn't, it should be modified. I want to buy fabrics that I like, of course; but I don't have to live with them. I want the client to see them, touch them, and be sure.

Most of my clients have already been stuffed with other people's ideas of what their homes should or shouldn't be like. My job, I believe, is to discover some of the clients' own long-buried ideas, to find out what they really need, want, and like.

The first step is to understand that in designing a home one is working with *space*—space defined by floors, walls, and ceilings. This is your space, and it's precious. Psychologically, your space is the arena in which you can be entirely yourself, in which you can move or rest as you please, in which your spirit can expand. If that seems a little abstract, look at it

another way. Space costs money. It's too valuable to waste.

Space by itself conveys a feeling of luxury. The grandeur of castles and cathedrals depends largely on vast, open interior space, space that evokes excitement and reverence.

Luckily, we really don't need or even want space on this fantastic scale in our homes. Most people would feel lonely living in, say, a twenty-room house all by themselves. They'd probably close off fifteen rooms. Grandeur is fine up to a point, but we are all a little bit like hobbits. We also like coziness. A small space doesn't necessarily make for a too-small home.

Nevertheless, 99 percent of the people I meet feel that they don't have enough space. They seem to agree with me that space is precious and a luxury. But if you look around their homes and ask a few questions, it turns out that they don't really put much value on space itself. They think that luxury depends on the things one puts *into* space. Luxury is furniture, bric-a-brac, carpeting, pictures, mirrors, appliances, and so on.

Our culture conditions us to think this way. And I respond like anyone else—no matter how hard I try, I still find that I buy and accumulate things that I don't really need or want. So I don't blame my clients for doing the same thing. But the first principle in successfully planning a home is: *Space itself is potentially as valuable as anything you can put into it.*

Don't start by thinking of "decorating" space, much less of just filling it up. Too many homes are overdecorated and overfilled with things people don't need and don't even see any more. What's worse, sometimes these things weren't even really desired

24

when they were bought. They were just the best that was readily available.

No matter what kind of home you live in or what your particular taste, the key to better living is planning. Plan your home to work efficiently for you. It doesn't matter if you live in a studio apartment, a duplex, a brownstone, or a suburban house, or whether your tastes incline to plain or fancy, modern or antique; there are certain functions your home should fulfill for you. Put your comfort and pleasure first, and plan for them. You'll find you're solving aesthetic problems as you go along.

Traditionally, the different functions of a home have been assigned to different rooms. Dining room for eating, parlor for entertaining, even sewing room for sewing, laundry room for ironing, and so on. Nowadays, not many people have so many rooms to work with. But even if they did, planning strictly on the basis of rooms can be a restricting and impractical approach. I ask people to try to relate their various needs to the *total* space in their homes. I myself think of a home as having private, or personal, space; semiprivate, or intimate, space (for family or close friends); and public space (for entertaining).

Not every functional unit of space needs to be defined by walls. Liberate yourself from the idea that room X is for eating and room Y for sleeping because the architect planned it that way, or because the other houses and apartments nearby are arranged that way. The best plan for a home might do away with some walls or build new ones, but it shouldn't be based on walls.

However, I'm not an enthusiast for radical structural changes unless necessary. In particular, I have a great respect for old houses and apartments, many of which were much more wisely and soundly built than what's going up today, and many of which have beautiful decorative features. I've seen good, old houses gutted, with walls and ceilings torn out, molding and trim stripped away—all mindlessly, and in pursuit of a chic modern look. Half the time (at least), if the old house had its problems, the modernized one has a lot more.

Probably the easiest way to conceive your total space is to imagine your home *minus everything* that's been put into it. There's almost always something exciting and appealing about an empty house or apartment, especially if it's freshly painted, the floors shine, and sunlight is coming in the windows. Haven't you had the experience of moving into a new, empty home with the feeling you'd make it perfect? Then, after a year or so, didn't it start to look a little cluttered? Complicated? Seem sort of cramped? Even gloomy or shabby? This has happened to almost everyone at some time. To rich people and poor ones, in small apartments and large houses.

If your home seemed more charming before you moved in, or if it hasn't turned out as you'd hoped, the best thing is to begin at the beginning. Mentally empty it, and start planning for what you really need and want. Swear that, in the end, nothing unnecessary or unloved will remain.

Don't worry if what you want can't be done or bought all at once. Even if it could be, this usually isn't the best way to design. Very experienced professionals have difficulty planning an entire home at one time. There are hundreds of details to be worked out. If you build little by little, what's done later can be modified to fit what went before. And you

25

don't want the initial plan to kill off your imagination. You should still be free to experiment and change your mind.

In thinking about your basic needs, you'll find that many are shared by almost everyone else in the world; they're virtually universal. Almost everyone needs and expects some kind of place to cook in a home. But what kind of place depends on whether you live alone or in a family, whether you love cooking or hate it, what kind of cooking you do, etc. Thus, ideally, each function should be met a somewhat different way in each individual home.

Little by little we'll get into discussions of how the use of various colors, shapes, styles of furniture, and other decorative features affect the character, or mood, of space and contribute to the total impression a home makes. But I always begin by thinking first about the basic needs a home must or, if possible, should meet. Some of them will seem terribly obvious, but I'm constantly surprised by how often apparently obvious needs are neglected or only partially met.

A home must provide shelter.

Most homes do at least this job adequately, but even here there are a few fairly common problems. Some popular architectural features are not well suited to the prevailing climate. This is more obvious now that most people want to cut down on costs of heating and air-conditioning. For example, picture windows (which I often enjoy) release heat in winter and act as radiators in summer. And in a city or suburb, a picture window is sometimes used as much by people looking in as by people looking out.

Also, as much as I love open space, a house with relatively small rooms, windows, and doors is easier to keep warm in a cold climate. I've been in newly built and renovated houses in New England having two-story living rooms that were very grand —and, in winter, very chilly. Heat does rise, so high ceilings work best in warm climates.

In contemporary suburban homes, the front door sometimes opens directly into the living room. Not only is this, psychologically, a very abrupt kind of entrance, but cold winds rush in. I've been in such rooms where I had to jump up and chase after newspapers every time someone opened the front door.

This book is not primarily intended for readers who're building from scratch or doing major structural renovation, but if you are, don't overlook the weather. Study the traditional architecture of the region; you don't have to copy it, but be sure you understand it. If certain architectural features and building materials have been used for a couple of hundred years, there may be some good reasons why.

There are cold materials that reflect away heat and warm materials that absorb it. The design of roofs and porches must take into account the possibility of heavy snow and rain. The low ranch house is excellent on a windy plain, not so good where there's a chance of flooding.

In cities, and sometimes even in suburbs and towns, you may need shelter against noise. This is as important to your well-being as keeping out cold. Carpeting or in other ways padding walls and ceilings is considered chic. But I don't do it just to be cute. It can make a noisy, unpleasant space quiet and comfortable.

A home should provide a comfortable place to sleep, wash, and dress for whoever lives there.

One of my clients lived in a studio apartment with a fold-out sofa bed. Every night for eighteen years, she unfolded the sofa, put away the cushions, and got her pillows. Every morning, she put away the pillows, and so on, in reverse. She called in a decorator who had elaborate plans for refurbishing. It didn't occur to either of them that the poor woman had no convenient place to lie down and go to sleep. They took it for granted that a studio apartment doesn't have a bedroom.

Well, I built her a bedroom, about seven by ten, with padded walls (as soundproofing) and an arched doorway. It has room for her desk-and-sewing-machine unit, so she can write or sew without having to clean up in the middle of a project because guests are due. The moral is: Don't pay attention to arbitrary rules about what your home is supposed to look like, if they interfere with your comfort.

Over and over, I've seen homes where someone or everyone was shortchanged on sleeping comfort.

Children are often squeezed together in a small room when there is a larger room or some other arrangement available. Naturally, the children fight with each other.

Couples sometimes sleep in the same room because it's supposed to show that they're happily married, when in fact they don't enjoy sleeping in the same room and it's interfering with their marriage.

Single people often sweep into their bedrooms all sorts of odds and ends they don't want out in the living room for visitors to see. Then they find their bedrooms depressing.

Psychologically, a bedroom is your most important personal space. People keep what is most intimate and valuable to them in the bedroom, including money, jewelry, personal papers, letters, photographs of loved ones. A bedroom should not only be comfortable, it should be comforting. But, paradoxically, many people don't enjoy their bedrooms. They go there only at night to sleep. They let the bedroom deteriorate, probably because it's seldom on show as other parts of the home are.

Whether a bedroom should be more than a personal place for sleeping depends on your tastes and needs. Historically, depending on the culture or a person's social class, the "bedroom," or sleeping area, has ranged from a mat on the floor, perhaps protected by a screen, to an elaborate chamber in which visitors were received. But most people actually prefer a small, cozy space for sleeping. Large bedrooms often had curtained and canopied beds, which not only kept out the cold but provided privacy and a sense of security.

For convenience, your sleeping place should be as close as possible to where you wash and dress. But there are numerous ways these areas can be related. Bathroom and dressing room can be combined. Or a dressing room can also be a personal parlor (a boudoir, for example) or a study. A bedroom can be opened up to include a bath or sauna.

In most homes, though, there is little variety. Typically, the main, or master, bedroom is overfurnished. Second, most bedrooms (except children's rooms) are underused. They're larger than they need be just for sleeping, but they're empty for more than two-thirds of the day. Oddly, some people will push a double bed into a corner of the room to open

27

up more (underused) space. They then have difficulty getting in and out of bed, climbing in from one end or over their spouses. And making the bed becomes a real chore.

Children's bedrooms are usually overused. Not only are the kids suppposed to sleep there, they're supposed to work there, play there, and sometimes entertain there. In many homes it would make sense to switch the main bedroom and the children's room, if the parents prestige could survive the blow.

The "use factor" is the key to planning a more effective allocation of space in a home. If you estimate for each area of your home how many people spend how much time there, you may discover a pattern of underuse and overuse that indicates the direction in which changes can be made.

In the case of bathrooms, the use factor often indicates a domestic crisis. In general, bathrooms aren't large enough and there aren't enough of them. Also, their design is so poor I could write a book on the subject, but there's a good one already: *The Bathroom* by Alexander Kira.

I like a bathroom that can be used for lounging and dressing, and so do most of my clients, but this can't always be arranged.

When sharing a bathroom is causing friction, I've sometimes been able to effect partial remedies by installing two sinks in place of one; or putting a sink in a bedroom (attractive sink/dressing table units are available or can be built); or partitioning off the toilet to form a "water closet"; or installing an extra toilet and a small basin elsewhere in the home. In desperation I've even considered building outhouses, but these are only popular among ecology buffs.

A home should have a convenient and comfort-able place for cooking and eating. Very many homes lack one or the other, and many lack both.

The kitchen is potentially the most sociable space in the home, the hub of family life and an intimate, informal place for entertaining friends. It's attraction is almost mythical. The cooking fire and hearth are deep-rooted symbols of comfort and safety. A kitchen draws in people. It's the most relaxing place to express oneself, perhaps because there's no pressure to talk. In a crisis you'll find people gathering in the kitchen for solace.

It's almost impossible to have a kitchen that's too large. Give a kitchen a chance and it will double as a dining room, nursery, cocktail lounge, TV room, place for doing homework and household accounts, sewing and laundry room, first aid dispensary, and kennel.

Therefore, practically no one has a large enough kitchen. There are three possible approaches to this problem.

Move the kitchen to a bigger room, if possible. I worked on a house in Nantucket for a family of five. Both parents loved cooking and entertaining, and their way of life was informal, warm, and honest. Their children liked to be with them in the kitchen and so did guests, including me. It was a pleasure and an education to watch those good meals being prepared. But, alas, this nice family was making do with a small kitchen. Luckily, they did have a larger room, a library, that was underused. This was turned into the kitchen, with seating for eight to ten and an open wood-burning fireplace, and everyone is living happily ever after.

A small kitchen, even as small as a closet, can sometimes be opened up or extended by building

If you don't have space for two bathrooms, two sinks will help. Adjustable downlight is more bearable than constant fluorescent brightness.

29

counters out into the adjacent space, and also by moving some of what's stored in the kitchen into this space. If possible, there should be a small place for informal eating just near the kitchen, even if other arrangements have to be made for a real dinner party.

I've had clients who enjoy cooking but have just about given up on it because their kitchens were so small. In this predicament, it's worth it to try to make changes. You may think it will look odd to have a counter or cabinets or even the refrigerator outside the kitchen, but it might work very well. And if the food is good, no one is going to care that the kitchen has come out of the closet.

Finally, if activities like homework or ironing are being done in a small kitchen, move them elsewhere. The kitchen isn't the ideal place for concentrating anyway. What's needed is another work area. It's particularly sad when a kitchen doubles as a woman's only private place in the home, and there isn't even an easy chair for her to relax in. If you're spending time in the kitchen not because you love it but because you've no other place of your own, the answer is to build a nook for yourself—maybe as far from the kitchen as possible!

Almost as often as people lack space in the kitchen, they waste it in the dining room. We're still hung up on the Victorian dining room, which works best when there are four or more people at dinner and a staff to cook and serve the food. But those days are gone forever. Moreover, the Victorian dining room has never been well suited to spontaneous, lively conversation. And it's a torture for young children; if you don't think so, try eating while your

legs are dangling in the air, and the table is raised up under your chin—and don't fidget.

If you have a traditional dining room, you will probably walk around that large table and that set of chairs at least 18,000 times every ten years. You may think you can't do without it, but probably you can. There are numerous alternatives. Here, for example, is one: "Standard Dining Room" is a plan of a dining room that will seat eight and not do much else. "Liberated Dining Room" will seat ten to twelve and can also be used for lounging, music, and study.

Usually I recommend permanent seating only for the number of persons who regularly eat together. For a single person or a couple, I prefer to set up a small table (seating two or three) by a window. Maybe you've noticed that in restaurants couples usually pick a window table if one's available. A view provides variety. Even the most passionate lovers want to look at something besides each other. Corner tables are also popular, because they give a sense of intimacy. They do the same in a home, and save space

For a family of four, I might build or buy two matching tables, each seating four, one of which can be used every day. If six or eight are coming to dinner, the tables can be placed end to end or next to each other, perhaps corner to corner. Or a dropleaf table seating eight (and preferably oval-shaped) can sometimes be kept conveniently against a wall for use when guests are invited.

For groups larger than six or eight, a number of small tables usually makes for a better dinner party than one large table. One of my clients, who entertains frequently and well in a fairly modest apartment, sets up tables for four and has them removed after

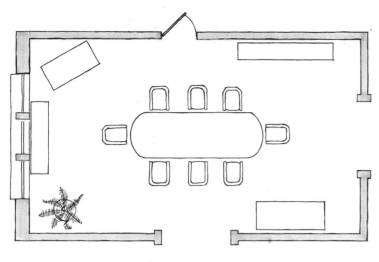

STANDARD DINING ROOM

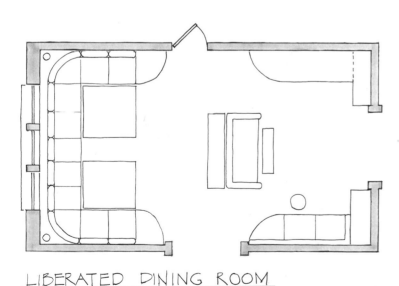

LIBERATED DINING ROOM

dinner. The last time I was there, we were twenty-four to dinner, and we ate very comfortably, and we had the use of all that space after dinner.

The reason I urge small tables and oval or round tables is to promote better communication and more fun for everyone. No more than five or six people can talk together easily—that is, with each person having a chance to say something, not just listen. With a small group it's hard not to be drawn in; in a large group it's easy to be left out. Undoubtedly your guests want to meet everyone at your parties, but not necessarily all at one time.

For a group of eight or more, an oval or round table is better than a rectangular one because it's easier for your guests to see and hear each other. It's also much easier to pass things. (I've built some round tables with Lazy Susans in the middle, so not much passing is necessary anyway.)

There's a rule of communication, which is obvious, but often ignored in dining rooms and living rooms. It is that people lined up in a row aren't going to be able to talk together very well. I've been at many formal dinners where it was only possible to talk to the person on my right and the person on my left, and not to both at the same time. To speak to someone across the table, I had to shout. To speak to someone two seats away I had to lean across a neighbor or lean back and talk behind his or her back. Meanwhile, we were all at the mercy of any bore with an urge to capture an audience.

Another unpleasant situation for a guest is to sit nervously with other guests while the host or hostess is running in and out of the kitchen, preparing the food, getting it on the table, clearing

31

If you're not eating breakfast because there's no place to sit in the kitchen, a small table nearby may solve the problem.

32

away dishes, etc. In planning a dining area, I usually ask clients to consider serving buffet style unless they plan to have hired help for the serving. With a buffet, you won't miss what's going on in the living room—or, maybe more important, what's not going on. A buffet also allows guests to eat what they want, more or less when they want it, and to continue conversations that are under way.

As for cleaning up after the meal, I recommend a trolley that will carry off a large load in one swoop.

The point of dining less formally is not to substitute raw convenience for old-fashioned graciousness but to adapt realistically to contemporary life. Theoretically, the old ways may seem more elegant. But if in fact the attempt to be formal results in a sense of strain and constraint, a more relaxed approach would be more hospitable.

You should also take a hard, realistic look at your daily eating habits. Some clients have told me that they've stopped eating breakfast because it's too much trouble to carry stuff to the table when they're rushed in the morning. Others complain that their children leave dinner as soon as possible or prefer to eat in their rooms. In such cases I try to create a convenient and comfortable eating area that will help solve the problem. To a great extent the solution involves finding the right furniture and creating pleasant lighting, but first an appropriate space has to be found: A place to eat in or near the kitchen, a corner where upholstered banquettes can be built, or whatever. Finding the space won't necessarily solve the problem—some people will never eat breakfast and some families are barely on speaking terms—but it's a first step.

In a home there should be a private place for each person who lives there—a place to relax, be alone, put up one's feet (very healthy), doze, read, listen to music.

A home without private places tends to be a home full of tensions. Usually a large studio apartment is not as satisfactory an arrangement for a couple as a smaller two- or three-room apartment. The presence of another person, even at some distance, imposes certain demands. No one is completely himself or herself while being observed. Each person has a different set of inhibitions, but we all have some. In front of another person we're always a bit on our good behavior, always somewhat sensitive to the other's reactions.

Possessive and insecure people are always jealous of others' privacy, with some reason. A person who's left the room and closed the door has stepped into his or her own world.

How much privacy a person needs depends on the individual, the other people around, and to some extent the cultural context. For example, in America "paper-thin" walls are a symbol of lack of privacy. In Japan, real paper walls can provide adequate privacy, the paper wall being regarded to some extent as inviolable.

In some American homes "father's chair" is similarly inviolable, or used to be. When father is in his chair, reading his paper and smoking his pipe, he's not to be disturbed. Respect for another's privacy can be more effective than simply having doors to shut.

If father doesn't have his own private spot, he needs one. Ditto for mother and children. Curiously,

33

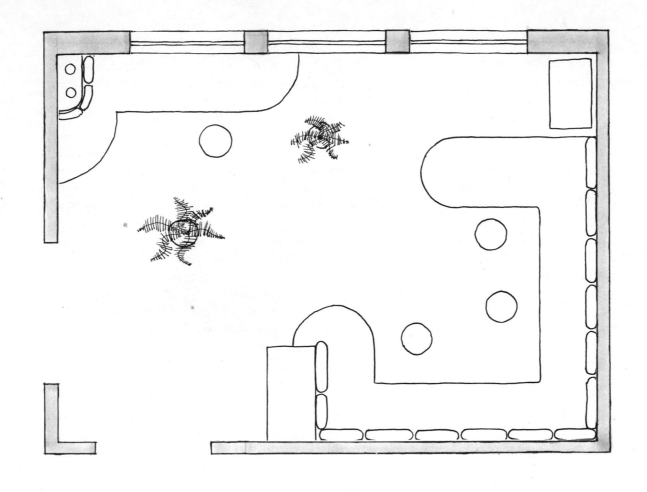

A PRIVATE PLACE

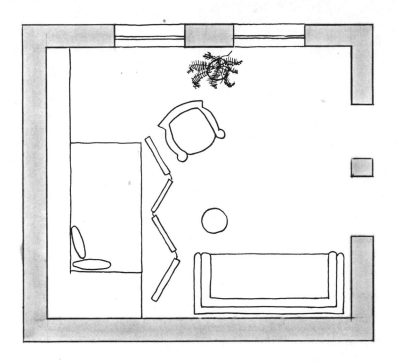

A VERY PRIVATE PLACE

many people aren't conscious of this need, although they'll go to strange lengths to fulfill it. Not infrequently I've found that people retreat to the john. This is hardly the answer, especially if you're short of bathrooms. Little children will hide behind a sofa or under the front porch or in a tree house, if they're lucky enough to have one. Older children who lack privacy may solve the problem by just not coming home.

Recently I was working with a young family in New York, and the husband was becoming grumpier and grumpier. His wife wanted her own place to work, and I was fixing up a desk for her in what previously had been exclusively a dining room. He started complaining that it wasn't practical, she'd take up too much room, and so on, and so on. It turned out that, although he hadn't mentioned it and really hadn't consciously thought about it, he had no comfortable place to relax in the evenings. He'd been using the bedroom, which gave him privacy all right but wasn't convenient for reading, listening to music, or smoking.

The solution was to build him his own place, shown on the far left. The banquette looks out over the Hudson. The pillows are designed so he can sit up and read or lie back and doze. There's a good light overhead that can be made bright or dim.

In this case, by simply orienting the space away from the main seating area and partially screening it off with plants, enough privacy was achieved for this man's needs. The next plan, "A Very Private Place," might be considered a little eccentric, but it's what the client wanted. The banquette is just a cushioned platform built in the corner of a small

35

A private space
should be totally
yours, drawn from
your own
fantasies. This
woman wanted her
space to be
glamorous and
seductive.

guest room. It's shielded by a screen and a daybed. Again, the pillows can be used for sitting up or lying down. Ordinarily I would fix it so you didn't have to crawl over a daybed to get into your own corner, but this woman wanted her place to be as inaccessible to her family as possible. Within this little nook, there are bookshelves, a telephone, and an adjustable light for reading.

In my own home, which is essentially a loft, I've made my bedroom into a private place. I didn't want to build walls, so I used fabric to create a kind of hallway and partition. Although there's no door at the entrance to my "hall," most people hesitate to go in without asking because the entrance is away from the main flow of traffic and has a slightly mysterious, secret feeling. Its placement discourages exploration.

Few family homes have enough rooms for everyone to have a private room to himself for studying, resting, or relaxing, but private places can be improvised within larger spaces once the need for them is realized.

Ideally, a home should have at least one semi-private, or intimate, area for close friends or family to be together. Such areas often evolve naturally, without planning. In a studio apartment there may be one corner where people usually sit, while the rest of the space is used for other purposes or when there's a party. In a large home, a small library may be used by the family or for small parties. In some homes, of course, the kitchen is the favorite gathering place.

Many middle-class families have a family "den," which is an excellent idea, often spoiled in practice. The most common problem is that the den isn't kept exclusively for the family. It's regularly invaded by guests.

Again and again I've visited in these homes and been escorted right past a perfectly good living room into the den, whereupon children in pajamas scatter to their rooms, fathers watching football groan quietly, and a nice Sunday has been spoiled.

A family area should be a place where anyone in the family can lie around in pajamas, read the paper, play a game, or whatever, without fear of interruption. Guests should be entertained in the living room, and if the living room somehow doesn't seem friendly enough, the answer is to make *it* more liveable, not to use the den instead. Most often it's the parents who sin by bringing in guests, but the rule applies to children, too. An adult shouldn't be stuck with entertaining a visiting child any more than a child should be required to entertain adults, or disappear.

I've been in a number of roomy and expensive homes that have no family space at all. The house or apartment is quite strictly divided into adults' space and children's space. In my experience, these are unhappy homes.

Where there isn't the room to have one area exclusively for entertaining and another area for the family, it's no contest as to which is more important. The space should be designed to meet family needs first. With good storage arrangements, and if it's easy to clean, it will do perfectly well for guests, too. There's nothing wrong with a living room that looks as if it's used. In fact it's a great improvement over

*A banquette for resting,
listening to music, and watching
the sun set over the Hudson
(which the cat could see if he
were a nature lover).*

*The entrance to a private space
should not provide a view of the
interior.*

39

the living room that looks as if it's never been used and is never supposed to be.

Another common problem with dens is that they aren't set up to allow a range of activities. Sometimes a TV set monopolizes the room. Or the only place to play a board game is right in front of the door where people need to get by. Or there isn't table or counter space for hobbies or writing letters. Or there isn't enough comfortable seating. For example, a family of four used the room shown in "Standard Den No. 1." As you see, the room centered on a single gathering area, which was dominated by the stereo and TV units. There was wasted space to the right of the entrance, and the tables on each side of the sofa took up space without doing anything but holding lamps. There were few surfaces for working or games. The coffee table was more obstructive than useful. There was little room for movement. The view (of Manhattan) was wasted.

In "Liberated Den No. 1," most of these difficulties have been resolved. The banquettes will together seat eight people (more than could be seated in the room before) and can be used for stretching out as well as sitting up. The platforms behind the banquettes (which are twenty-eight inches high) can be used as tables or as seating for a child. In this case, the platform near the window is used as a seat, the one to the left now holds a smaller television set. Substituting small tables for the coffee table allows more room for movement or just lying around on the floor. A counter-top desk has been placed to the right of the entrance with bookshelves behind it, with an aquarium on the top shelf. A turntable and records are on open shelves, and the speakers are

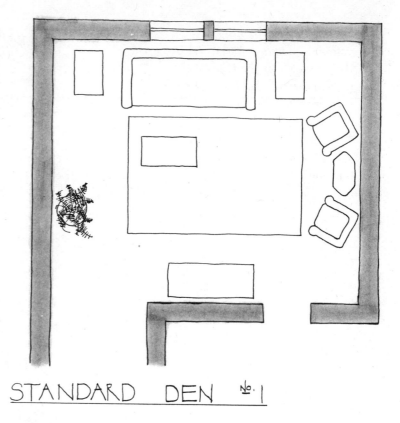

STANDARD DEN No. 1

LIBERATED DEN No. 1

under the banquettes, which I don't usually recommend, but these clients were into soul music and wanted to "feel" every note, literally.

You may have noticed that there's still some vacant, nonfunctional space directly in front of the main entrance. The reason is that a passageway has to be left to allow free access to the doors leading to the bedrooms and kitchen. This room has at least one door too many, but none of the doors could be closed off. It points up an important lesson, though. Doors eat up space, not just the space necessary to open them and get through them, but passage space required for a free approach. I once worked on a living room that had five doors, which is great for a French farce but not for much else. The room was 10 percent living space, 90 percent passage space.

If at all possible, there should be space in a home for play—for hobbies, games, exercises.

Most of us spend most of our time doing things others want done. At home you should be able to do what interests you and in your own way. And you should be able to move at home, not just sit down and lie down. Do you have room to turn a somersault or do the Hustle? If not, you may not need more space; you may need less furniture.

Most people realize that it's essential for children to have space for projects, hobbies, and exercise; they know a child learns and grows by trying different activities. But adults are learning and growing, too, although they tend to be stunted as a result of living in deprived environments, namely their own homes, where there's nothing for them to do but watch TV.

I meet many people taking "courses." They're

41

paying lots of money for lessons in painting, pottery, karate, photography, woodwork, sculpture, dancing, you name it. But they go *out* for their courses. At home they're very unadventurous. Paint or clay might harm the carpets. A punching bag wouldn't match the bedroom décor. They're also shy. They don't want to display their hobbies, for fear their work will seem too amateurish or their collections won't interest anyone else. So the hobby is hidden or abandoned because there "isn't enough room" for it.

Actually, though, almost any room can be used for a hobby. There is far more charm in an informal home where there's evidence of enthusiasm for *something* than in a sterile, careful home where everything's store-bought.

Don't hide your interests. Put them on display. They'll give your home that "creative personal touch" that so many advertisers refer to when they're trying to sell you some mass-produced gimmick.

Storage space is essential in all homes. In almost all homes there doesn't seem to be enough, and what there is is inconvenient. This isn't necessarily the fault of architects and designers. The average person could move into an empty warehouse and fill it up in two years. I've seen it get to the point where people are actually afraid to put things away for fear they'll never find them again. And some things seem to just lose themselves. For example, I often ask clients for a tape measure, and it's always supposed to be in the drawer with the knives or the sewing box or some other specified place, but it usually isn't. Tape measures, scissors, pliers, flash-

lights, warranties, and bankbooks can all disappear faster than Houdini.

Storage space needs as much thought and regular attention as the rest of the home. But it seldom gets it, probably because guests don't have to be shown the closets.

Some kinds of storage spaces aggravate the tendency of things to get lost. Chests and deep drawers are convenient only for keeping a few bulky items, such as blankets. Fill them with smaller items, like sweaters and scarves or papers and photographs, and unless what you want is right on top, you won't find it easily. And while you dig around, you make more of a jumble.

High shelves work best for things that can be identified at a glance, such as suitcases. Anonymous cartons and shopping bags just gather dust up there and give you guilt. Do try to find out what's in your closets. You'll probably discover things that can be thrown away or stored more efficiently, thus opening up space you didn't know you had.

Clothes closets are usually inefficiently designed but also poorly used. Most people jam in too many clothes and then work from the middle of the pole. All the clothes get wrinkled, and those at the ends of the pole get lost. (This is where you'll find clothes you never liked or grew too fat or thin for years ago.) Shoes that are unfashionable or uncomfortable travel to the backs of closets. A shoe rack will free space for other things and keep the shoes in better shape.

In kitchens, high shelves and deep drawers and cabinets collect unused equipment, strange foods, and rare cleaning substances. Utility closets are usually a tangle of vacuum cleaner hose, mop handles, and ironing board legs. Pull out one thing and you get them all. Old rags lurk in the corners.

Attics, basements, and garages attract items that might some day appeal to antiquarians but probably are of no more use to you.

Obviously, one reason so many people are short of storage space is they're saving things they should get rid of. Another is that "putting away" has become confused with "hiding away." This is particularly true in kitchens, dens, and studies. In analyzing storage problems, one of the first things I look for is the possibility of getting stuff that is used fairly often (or could be) out into easy view and reach.

Lately, with the fashion for European cooking and European-style kitchens, people are somewhat more willing to let knives and pots all hang out, so to speak. But there's still a great reluctance to expose common products, such as canned goods, to the light of day. People will go to museums and look at Andy Warhol Campbell's soup cans, but they're embarrassed to have them out in their own kitchens.

The same goes for games in the family area or den. Games are a wonderful pastime, but usually they're stacked up on a closet shelf where they're forgotten. Games can be set out on their own shelf, and if they are, they'll be used more.

Sometimes the concept of "open storage" is hard to sell. A valid objection is that things that are left out get dusty and grimy, especially in cities. But if the objects are used regularly, this isn't a problem. And I notice that people set out spices, which they use up slowly, while shutting away corn flakes, which they use up quickly. Chess sets are displayed (and dusted) while checker sets are kept in the closet. So

sometimes it's convention as much as convenience that determines what's left out and what's shut away. I like to put a little more emphasis on convenience.

If things are going to be kept behind doors, they should at least be easy to see and reach when you want them. In kitchens, I sometimes make cabinet doors of clear acrylic. And large doors are often more functional than small doors. If I see that a client has to open three or four cute little doors in order to find the baking soda or honey, I start planning to to make larger doors.

If you have pots and pans stacked on top of each other under the sink or in some other inconvenient spot, consider a professional kitchen: The pots hang up in easy reach. You can buy ceiling fixtures in a variety of shapes (circles, rectangles, etc.) for holding them. I know some people are ashamed of their pots, but the only good reason to be ashamed is if you're showing off pots you don't use (which is sometimes done). I've had clients object that until they have more copper utensils they don't want their pots out. Copper is good to cook with, but the way it tarnishes, especially in the city, it's one type of kitchenware I'd rather *not* keep out.

Don't hang up pots where you'll walk into them, or over the stove, where they get greasy. Over a counter is usually the best place.

Do you have a couple of drawers jammed with large spoons, knives, whisks, roasting forks, measuring cups, etc.? Such drawers are very common and very inconvenient. They're bad for knives; the blades get dull and nicked. And small items, such as measuring spoons, get lost under larger ones. Hooks and magnetic holders will hold most of these.

I often build narrow shelves for items used frequently—spices, soups, cereals, pet food, kitchen silverware, plates, and glasses. I don't recommend commercial spice racks. Each household uses different kinds and amounts of spices. A standardized rack doesn't provide for this and is costly as well. Build a shelf that suits your own cooking.

Near the kitchen or dining room table (whichever is used more frequently), you can keep a day or two's worth of glasses, dishes, and flatware. I often put glasses on an open shelf, just one glass deep. For cups I use traditional hooks, which saves space and looks nice, too.

Flour, pasta, rice, cookies, sugar, and so on can be stored in glass containers. Glass is decorative and easy to wipe down. For the cheapest containers check your local restaurants and bars. Some of their supplies may come in large glass jars that they're just throwing out.

As for the utility closet, if it's a mess, see if you can hang brooms and mops on wall clamps—if not in the closet, then behind the kitchen door, at the top of the cellar steps, or the like. There may be room to add racks or a shelf to the inside of the closet door to hold polishes and soaps.

In most clothes closets, especially men's, there's relatively too much hanging space compared to shelf space, and even the hanging space isn't well planned. Often where there's only one rod, two will fit, one on top of the other. (Your longest garment determines the height needed for the bottom rod.) The top rod can be used for out-of-season clothes. If the closet is deep, you may be able to fit one rod behind another.

In or near the closet it's useful to have shelves for shirts, sweaters, blouses, lingerie, undershorts, socks, and so on. Men, I find, often prefer to keep shirts and undershorts just on an open shelf. But if you want to protect the clothing, lots of stores, including Woolworth's, sell neat plastic boxes in all sizes and shapes for everything from handkerchiefs to hats. I know women who've had hats hidden on closet shelves for years, permanently obscured in tissue paper or unlabeled boxes.

Sometimes a closet can be extended by removing the door and building shelving that extends from one wall of the closet and then turns at a right angle to face the closet entrance. A screen or partition can be used to hide the shelving, or the shelving can be "two-faced," forming on the other side a bookcase or bulletin board (for children's rooms) or whatever is needed most.

The point is to get your clothes all into one place, so you can dress easily in the morning. I usually ask clients if they can find what they want to wear when they're in a hurry. One honest woman told me no, she wears what she can find.

A central linen closet for a family is hard to keep neat, especially if more than one person handles the linen. I try to keep a two-or three-week supply of sheets and towels in the areas where they'll be used. To get a child to change his bed isn't ever easy, but it helps if the sheets are stored near his bed. It's also gracious to have an extra supply of towels in a bathroom a guest may use. Different colored sheets and towels for different rooms makes it simple to know what goes where.

If you have a basement, attic, or garage, you can organize an almost unlimited amount of storage, undoubtedly more than you need to have. Usually these wonderful places are badly neglected, and if a client can afford renovation, I hate to see them used just for storage. I try to create more living space.

Coping with closets, shelves, cabinets, files, and drawers is the least glamorous part of a designer's job, but extremely important. The storage arrangements have to work if any design is going to make sense. You can't start making plans for a space until you have some notion of what has to be stored in it and where. You can't design the "center" of a space, so to speak, while the periphery is lined with jumbled and overflowing cabinets, closets, and bureaus. Sooner or later, stuff is going to ooze out of those closets and spoil the room.

A home should have attractive and comfortable space for entertaining.

I've left this almost to the last, because it's truly more important that your home suit you first, guests second. But, typically, the most effort and money goes into the living room. It's the showplace of the home, the place where people express their ambitions and sense of their own worth.

Sometimes a home will deteriorate badly without anyone consciously noticing or minding until the living room starts to go. Then all of a sudden the whole place is "a wreck."

But, curiously, despite all this concern, living rooms are often the ugliest and least comfortable areas in the home.

A few years ago in Florida, I went on a round of holiday visits among Greek families living there. All the living rooms, or parlors, were basically the same. They were used only on special occasions. They contained almost exactly the same furniture, namely, a sofa (against one wall), with matching end tables (each holding a lamp); a large coffee table in front of the sofa; two matching chairs on either side of the coffee table, with matching little tables beside them. The rest of the chairs were placed against other walls.

Except for the four or five people sitting in or next to the sofa, the visitors were strung out around the edges of the room. If you were sitting on the sofa, and wanted to talk to someone across the room, it was quite a feat to maneuver around the coffee tables (each holding a lamp); a large coffee table in the room. Then either you both stood or one sat while the other stood, unless someone was nice enough to give up his chair and move, too, so you could sit next to your friend. The entire setup seemed designed to discourage spontaneity.

The rooms these families used every day, particularly the dens, or "rec" rooms, were much more inviting and warm, even though the furniture was old and the rugs were threadbare. But these people had never been encouraged to extend the good ideas they had for informal relaxing to the more formal rooms.

Of course, it's easy to be smug about the mistakes made by unsophisticated people, but more sophisticated people make the same mistakes. I've been in rooms, pure Louis XV or perfect American Colonial, that were just as unimaginative and uncomfortable— even more so, if you stopped to think what it would cost you to replace anything that might break. A cliché is a cliché, whether it's been promoted in *Good Housekeeping* or *Antiques Quarterly*.

Your entertainment space should give you the most chance to experiment and be the most fun to

45

create. Here you can think more about your likes than your needs. If you have a favorite color you can use it, without worrying how it will wear day in and day out. The space isn't going to be lived in day in and day out. But you do have to give some thought to the kind of spatial organization that enables a group of people to meet, communicate, move around, and mix easily.

A common worry among people who want to give big parties, for fifty or more, is that they don't have enough *total* entertaining space. But total space is seldom a problem. An amazing number of people can squeeze together, especially if they're willing to stand up in a crowd, and often they are. In a crowd it's easy to meet and start talking to new people. It's actually more awkward when a large space is only half or two-thirds full. Then guests break into isolated groups and wonder why more people didn't come to the party.

If you like to give big parties, nonfragile furniture helps, unless you don't mind some damage. Flimsy structures—such as commercial room dividers, which create bottlenecks and make people nervous—have to go.

For food and drinks it's best to have a large table (or perhaps two) preferably placed away from the wall, so that guests can approach from all sides rather than waiting in a line or a clump. If you don't have an appropriate table, a collapsible metal one will do, or even a large piece of plywood on sawhorses. With a tablecloth no one can see what's underneath.

If there's seating for half the guests, that's plenty. You don't want the people standing up to look like the losers at musical chairs. There's no need to move furniture out of the middle of the room.

People enjoy finding their own territories. If you have a chair near a wall with room for only one person behind it, then you can push it back. Or you can pull it out, so that two can fit behind it.

If there's not a big room for guests' coats, then a coatrack in the hall will prevent jam-ups at the end of the evening.

For clients who entertain, I always try to arrange enough space for dancing. This isn't necessary if you're certain that neither you nor any of your friends would never dance under any circumstances. But personally, I love dancing, and think it's the quickest, most exciting way to bring a party to life.

I build platforms for dancing that can be disassembled and stored in a closet. They needn't be big; I find that eight people can dance in about the space taken up by a dining room set. And although I often dislike coffee tables, I've built one I love: It's oversize and doubles as a dancing platform.

In designing for entertaining, there are two fundamentals: allowing for communication and creating easy flow, or movement. The larger the group, the fewer the channels of communication. In a large classroom, the teacher talks and the students listen. If the teacher tries for open discussion, the results are usually just noisy.

If you watch a large group, you'll see that it tends to break into smaller units. And these groups in turn tend to break up and re-form, if there's room for the people to move around. You don't have to force it (some people maniacally push reluctant guests from one group to another); it will happen if you provide the right kind of space.

Remember that easy communication doesn't take place among people all sitting in a row. A sofa against

46

a wall with no chairs nearby can be used comfortably only by two people, even if it seats three. Even more useless is a single chair, or even a pair of chairs, against a wall. This is an arrangement that breeds wallflowers.

It should be possible for two or three persons to leave one conversation and move easily to a place of their own centered on other chairs, a window seat, a pouf, or whatever. (This can, by the way, save a party, if two guests have taken a dislike to each other.) And the conversation areas should be balanced.

Sometimes a room is overweighted on one side or at one end. There's space for people to move into, but it's empty and not enticing.

Entertainment space shouldn't be so overfurnished that you feel trapped wherever you happen to be. It also shouldn't be "static," which is difficult to define but refers to a structure that "feels" rigid, that discourages natural, or organic, movement. What it usually boils down to is too much symmetry and too many right angles. A slightly curving, or sinuous, line is often more pleasing, just as it's more pleasing to drive on a somewhat curving and hilly road than on an endless straightaway.

Let's look at a couple of specific examples. In "Standard Living Room No. 1," the design is compulsively symmetrical. There isn't enough seating. Only four can sit comfortably on the two sofas; the chairs on either side of the breakfront could be carried over near the sofas, but in that position they'd completely block up the room; however, they're no use to anyone where they are now. Thus, there's only one, limited, conversation area.

Here, redesigned as "Liberated Living Room

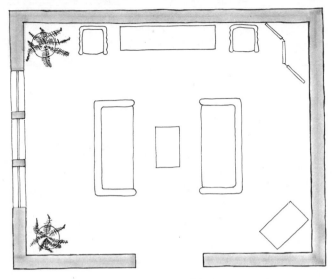

STANDARD LIVING ROOM №. 1

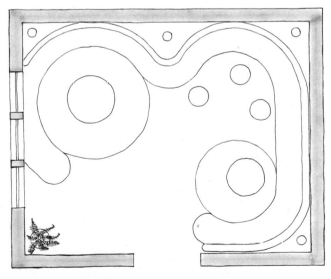

LIBERATED LIVING ROOM №. 1

47

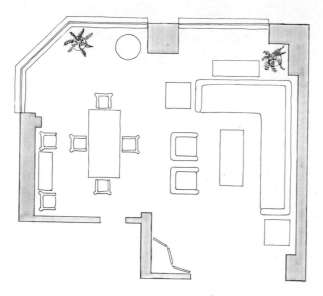

STANDARD LIVING ROOM №2

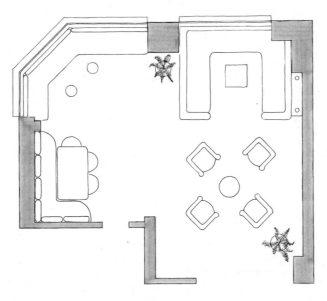

LIBERATED LIVING ROOM №2

No. 1," the same space has two, and potentially three, interrelated conversation areas. There's more variety in the shapes and a more dynamic arrangement. Also, there's considerable free space. If this room belonged to a family that was short of informal family space, the spare corner could be used for games or TV watching; a desk or hobby table could be set in another corner.

In "Standard Living Room No. 2," you can see many of the same problems as in No. 1, and in addition a good view is wasted, which happens incredibly often. In "Liberated Living Room No. 2," the view is now part of the room. There are two conversation areas, and the swivel chairs give at least two people the choice of either talking with the group around the sofa or being in a separate group. The room will now seat sixteen easily, but there's still space for a desk or table in the left-hand corner. The banquette by the bay window can be used for napping or reading. The low table in front of the banquettes would be, if designed by me, tough enough to serve as a footrest as well as a coffee table.

There are two special situations that cause real difficulties if you like to entertain: One is when your space is very, very small. The other is when it's very large.

In a small space, keep the furniture to a minimum, and don't push it all back against the walls. This emphasizes the limits of the space—namely, the walls—and makes the room seem boxlike. Instead, work against the walls, using angles and curves to de-emphasize them.

The plans here are based on a job I did in a very small two-room apartment in the Bronx. Incidentally, the cost of the living room was only $450. (Like any

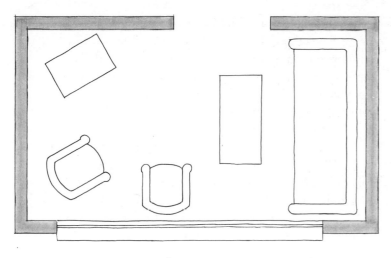

TINY L.R. (BEFORE)

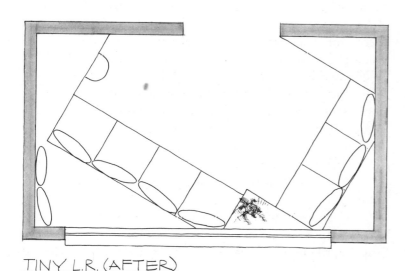

TINY L.R. (AFTER)

designer, I feel sure I can do good work when the client has plenty of money. But I like to think my ideas can be adapted to any budget.)

Anyway, "Tiny Living Room (Before)" is the plan of a room eight by fourteen feet, which is jammed with furniture but seats only four. The view from the window is wasted. The plan for "Tiny Living Room (After)" is based on banquettes set at angles. The spaces behind the banquettes are to be used either for sitting or as tables. The long banquette will seat five, the shorter one, three. Notice that the pillows are set at an angle so that they slightly face each other, rather than being in a straight line. And, of course, one can stretch out on these banquettes, which was impossible in the previous design. There's still room for a desk with a lamp. Other lighting is provided by overhead fixtures.

In a very large space the problem is to provide continuity between conversation areas and variety in shapes and colors. The prototype of a poor design is the baronial hall, where everyone crowds into a small space around the fireplace while the rest of the room recedes into chilly, vacant gloom. In a vast space, such as a loft, simply spreading around interesting furniture won't create an inviting atmosphere. Two approaches that help to break up the space effectively are to build on different levels and to introduce large sculptures or elements of nature, such as a fountain, hanging panels or sculptures, or a grouping of plants and trees. The aim is to arrange areas where four or six people can gather cozily. Ideally, the remaining open space should form an intriguing configuration, such as a "Z."

Last, but very far from least, a home should be easy to clean.

Even if you can afford and want hired help to do all the cleaning, it's hard to find skilled cleaners these days. If your home isn't easy to clean, it probably will seldom be clean. If you do some or all of your own cleaning, a hard-to-clean home is a burden that you may come to dislike no matter how beautiful it is.

A critical factor in ease of cleaning is the amount of surface area to be coped with. An empty room isn't hard to clean. Fill it up with furniture and other objects, and very soon the total surface area of the things in the room will exceed the total area of the walls, ceiling, and floor. Each unnecessary object creates unnecessary work. There's a good name for this kind of object: dust-catcher.

Analyze your movements when you clean. How many separate things do you have to move or pick up? How many pieces of furniture have to be cleaned? Can you and your vacuum cleaner move through your rooms easily, or do you have to push aside the furniture to get into the corners? Are there places you can't get to at all? And, finally when you're finished, does the room look bright and neat or still sort of dull and littered? Would it help to get rid of some things?

By this time, you probably get the idea that I'm a fanatic about clutter. It's true. It's by far the most common and incurable problem I meet. It often begins the day a person moves into a home and gets progressively worse. It seems to sneak in with the morning mail and spread. It's depressing and demoralizing.

The last time I moved, I'd been in my home about six weeks when I found two cartons I still hadn't unpacked. I couldn't imagine what was in them. Everything I needed and everything I liked was already in place. I finally decided if I'd lived happily for six weeks without whatever was in those cartons, I wasn't going to open them. I just put them out with the garbage. I still can't believe I really did it, but I haven't regretted it yet.

Of course, there are some people who really enjoy Victorian complexity, loads of furniture, and dozens of *objects* in every room. This is a style in its own right, and it is sometimes carried off very well. But ninety-eight times out of a hundred, clutter isn't deliberate or artful. It's an unfortunate accident.

When I'm considering the potential of the total space in a home, there are two general goals I keep in mind and try to explain to my clients. One is good traffic flow and the other is flexibility.

Designing for traffic flow in a home is something like designing for traffic on streets and roads. One takes into account the total volume of traffic, the need for appropriate entrances and exists, direct versus indirect approaches, best routes, restricting traffic, and so on.

This may seem rather abstract, but the process isn't that complicated. I observe patterns of how people move in a home to see what problems there are. You can do this youself.

First, if you have hallways, are they clear? They should be. Hallways are meant to provide easy passage.

This seems terribly obvious, but it's surprising how often halls are obstructed. Furniture is usually the culprit, but bicycles, low-hanging light fixtures, baby carriages, and other stray obstacles are also common hazards. After a while you probably don't even notice the problem.

I look to see if a person can get through a hallway, even while carrying packages or a baby, without having to slow down or turn sideways.

Near the front door there should be room for people to say hello and goodby, take off and put on coats, without danger of being struck in the head by a chandelier or hat rack or tripped by an umbrella stand.

Is there a hall table? Does it create a bottleneck? Hall tables tend to collect mail, newspapers, hats, gloves, scarves, schoolbooks, dog leashes—even large objects like briefcases and musical instruments. If there's no hall table, there's no temptation to dump stuff on it, no need to stop in front of it, no need to edge around it. I regard hall tables with some suspicion. Often they're not useful at all.

Are there bookcases in the halls? Do they take up too much space? Are they ever used? Frequently it's difficult to see the books in a hall bookcase (it's too dark) or there isn't room to stand back and read the titles), so the books are forgotten.

The scatter rug can be a menace in halls and elsewhere. Do you slow down whenever you approach one for fear of tripping? Do you take guests by the arm to get them safely across the rug? Why do you have such a rug? If you love it, hang it on a wall. It will last longer, and so may you.

Sometimes halls are so difficult to navigate that people avoid them and take alternate routes. I worked in one home where there was a perfectly good hall connecting the bedroom wing of the apartment with the dining room and kitchen. The hall ran past the living room and the study, and there were double doors leading from hall to living room. Since the hall had become a storage place (jammed with bicycles, boxes, paintings, and sculpture), everyone in the family had stopped using it. To get from their bedrooms to the kitchen, the kids would walk straight through the living room and study. This wasn't good for the parents and their friends, who couldn't get away from the parade of children. And it wasn't good for the children either. Every time they passed their parents, questions were apt to come up like, "Didn't you *just have* a sandwich?" or "Have you finished your homework yet?" It was a perfect setup for nagging and fights.

The solution was to clear out the hall (the bicycles were hung on the wall) and close off the double doors (creating more living space in the living room).

Other passageways that are often neglected are secondary staircases: back stairs, basement stairs, and attic stairs. There must be special homicidal fiends who build back stairs as dark, steep, and slippery as possible (of course, traditionally these were used by mere servants). Most secondary staircases need to be relit and repaired, with treads or carpeting added or fixed. What usually happens, though, is that the stairs are just used less and less and never fixed up because no one uses them. Then one day someone does use them, falls down, and goes to the hospital. It's cheaper to fix the stairs.

Each entranceway and door should get individual attention. These are the valves that control and encourage or discourage traffic. As I've mentioned, a door may be unnecessary, a space-waster that creates

51

An uncluttered hallway.

52

a traffic lane where there isn't or needn't be traffic. So for each door, I ask, is it used? is it needed? is it appropriate to the room?

An odd thing I've noticed is that some people will automatically use the front door even when the back door is more convenient. In many apartments and houses there's a back door leading directly into the kitchen, but whoever's bringing home the groceries will still use the front door, and tote packages though a couple of rooms to get to the kitchen. Sometimes, usually in the country, the pattern is reversed. The back door is used constantly—even when there are guests, and the front door is just as accessible and more attractive.

Thus, designers learn the hard way that a logical plan isn't necessarily the best plan. Each person uses a home a different way.

To make guests welcome the entrance to the living room should be wide and inviting, encouraging people to enter. But this doesn't mean there has to be a straight passage from front door, through foyer, right to the center of living room. On the contrary, this kind of approach is aesthetically uninteresting and can make the living room itself seem smaller. I often set up "teasers" to partially block the full view of a living room. Large plants or potted trees or sculpture can be used. Sometimes the shape of the room and the arrangement of the furniture does the job.

The principle of a teaser is the same one used by "exotic" dancers. What can be seen all at once isn't as exciting as what's revealed little by little.

If the front door opens directly into the living room, it's particularly important to have a teaser,

not only for interest but to block drafts. I've used screens of tinted, semitranslucent glass or plastic, banks of plants, or a partition with paintings, drawings, or photographs.

Double doors or outsize doorways often form the entrances to living rooms and dining rooms. They're psychologically appropriate, but they sometimes raise practical problems. Double doors that swing open require a lot of space. Often there's furniture in the way. I know one family with double doors between the living room and dining room who over the years amassed so much furniture in the vicinity of the doors that only one could be opened, and that for only about eighteen inches. The family would squeeze through sideways; when guests came they'd move some furniture so the door would open a little wider. In such cases, the thing to do is either close off the doors entirely or remove them.

On the other hand, an outsize entrance without doors can mean loss of privacy for those in the living room or problems with heating or air-conditioning the room. The solution may be glass-paned doors (for a feeling of openness) or tinted-glass doors (for privacy).

Between the kitchen and dining areas easy access is essential, and a door may be more trouble than it's worth. If you do feel you need a door, you may find one made partly of glass more practical than a solid one. When more than one person is helping with the table, kitchen doors—especially swinging ones—get in the way, or worse, hit people in the nose. At least with glass you have a chance to duck.

A plain counter separating the kitchen and din-

53

ing area is often a pleasant and convenient arrangement. I have this in my own home. The counter partially shields the view of the kitchen and is a good place for working and serving. Guests can bring over dishes and glasses without having to squeeze through a door one by one and without getting in the way of the cook.

In some parts of a home the main problem isn't to ease traffic but to restrict it. Access to bedrooms and studies should almost always be very limited. In particular, parents' bedrooms should be at a dead end, if possible, and not adjacent to heavily used rooms or hallways.

Too many parents' bedrooms become extensions of the nursery. Others look as if they were designed primarily to make a good impression on elderly cousins and visiting clergy.

Grown-ups' bedrooms should be sexy, and you shouldn't have to worry about whether a child is going to walk in or listen in. In fact, once a child is old enough that you're more worried about whether he can hear you than whether you can hear him, it's time to move the bedrooms apart, if possible. If not, soundproofing may be in order. And there should be strict rules, locks if necessary, to discourage unexpected visits. Most children will accept this, if parents are also careful about not barging into the children's rooms.

In the home I worked on in Nantucket, where we turned the library into the kitchen, the parents were constantly aware of the children around, even when they were alone in their own bedroom. Luckily, there was an attic. It was a mess and hard to get to (but that was part of the point). We redesigned it as

54

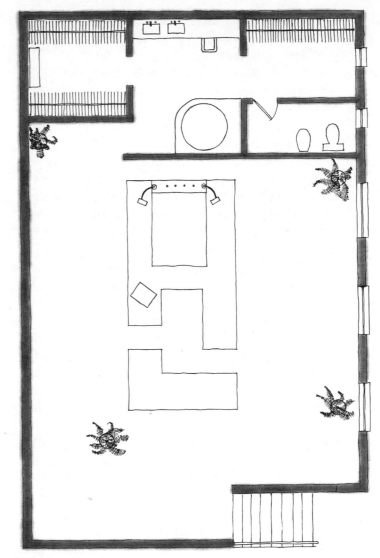

ATTIC BEDROOM

a bedroom and private living room for the parents. Children welcome on invitation only.

Here's a plan of the room. The window looks out over the Atlantic. There's a skylight overhead, between the bed and the window. The bed unit and separate banquette are essentially platforms set on bronze legs, upholstered in quilting material. The mattress is recessed in the frame. The room is studded with lights of different colors that can be dimmed or raised; there are lights under the platforms. A TV sits at the foot of the bed, on the left. Behind the bed there are two reading lights and a light panel, which also controls the TV. The bathroom has two sinks, a dressing table, a round tub, and a separate toilet/bidet room. It's a place for parents not to be parents for a while.

If children don't have privacy in their own rooms, I try at least to find some lounging space for them where they can be alone. In a split-level suburban home where I worked recently, not only were the bedrooms of the parents and three children crowded together, but the parents' living room and the children's playroom were separated only by a staircase. Naturally, neither room was really enjoyed —too much noise flowed back and forth. In this case, I moved the children's playroom into the garage, which was quiet and out of the way. The father agreed that people were more important than cars and moved the cars under a breezeway. The old playroom became a family den and TV room. The living room is used for guests or when the parents want to be alone.

I haven't heard that the cars are any the worse for the experience.

Finally, *within* rooms there should be room for free movement, but how much space is necessary for this purpose depends on the function of the room. A study can seem quite cramped and actually be just right for the one person who uses it. More empty space must be left in a living room, which is used by groups of people. But what most people do is fill up each room approximately to the same degree. They're judging by eye (and usually overfilling), without consideration of how the room will be used. In fact, they're more apt to stuff a living room with furniture on the theory that it will make a better impression and be more comfortable.

If you're lucky enough to have a kitchen that can accommodate any traffic at all, then you should give special consideration to the most functional arrangement. Sometimes the best design for a kitchen requires centering the main work units. For example, on the next page is the plan of a very nice kitchen I wish I had. It's from that favorite home of mine in Nantucket. The central unit contains a sink (that can be approached from two sides), oven, open charcoal broiler, dishwasher, and counter. Shelves and the refrigerator are to the left and right. The table in front of the fireplace will seat eight. It's a wonderful room to be in.

The other general goal I mentioned was flexibility. This has two related aspects: the potential of space for multiple-purpose use and the nonspecialization of space.

Flexibility is almost always essential to apartment living. Except in very large apartments, rooms have to serve more than one function. Usually, as I've said, the rooms that can best serve a second function

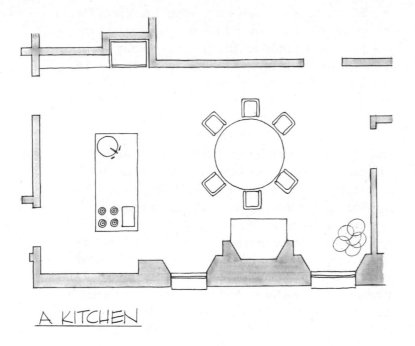

A KITCHEN

are bedrooms and dining rooms. For example, in designing this bedroom, the main problem was that he liked to watch TV, while she watched less but liked to knit. The bed acts as a kind of partition. There's a love seat at the end of the bed facing the fireplace and the TV. He can sit here with his feet up on the table. (There's room for her to join him, of course.) At the opposite end of the room, she has an easy chair and a table with a good light. Over the bed hangs a tinted cut glass disk, four feet in diameter. This helps to filter out the glare from the different light sources and create a little more privacy.

Luckily this couple doesn't have a problem with one wanting to go to bed earlier than the other. If they did, this design wouldn't work for them.

For space to work more than one way, or have the capacity to work more than one way, it mustn't be too specialized. People often don't understand it when I say: Don't overdesign, don't overdecorate. But if a space is made for a single mode and a single use, it may be wasted most of the time.

Flexibility is extremely important when children are in a home. When they're little the home has to be child-proofed to a certain extent. Floors and walls should be easy to clean; things the child can reach to break, tear, or poison himself with have to be raised out of reach; and so on. As the children get older, these arrangements can be relaxed but others have to be made. The children need more private places or quiet places for homework. Later, they may need space to entertain friends. The home should be able to change as the needs of the children change.

But it's not just children who change, although they do it most dramatically. All of us are changing all the time, although we may not perceive it so

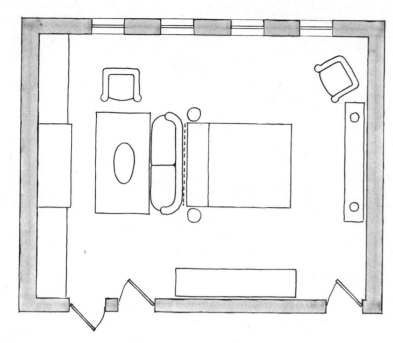

A BEDROOM FOR TWO

clearly. One year we may do a lot of entertaining, the next we may spend more time working at home. We change jobs, friends, lovers, and—alas, spouses. Each new situation brings different needs and different ideas, enthusiasms, likes, and dislikes.

In planning your home give yourself a chance to grow, try new things, have different moods. Don't try to fill every corner at once. Take your time and plan first for what you know you need. Let the rest of your space remain neutral for a while. You'll find uses for it soon enough. Don't lock yourself into limited themes, limited moods, limited activities.

Your home is your space, your place, to be yourself—not just the self you are right now, the self you're becoming as well.

SPACE PLANNING AND AESTHETICS

The home design business is full of specialists. There are architects and contractors, designers and decorators, landscape planners and plumbers. There are even consultants for your *indoor* plants, kitchen experts, and color counselors.

When I was beginning this book, a friend showed me the memoirs of a man who went West with his family back in the 1880s. On the way, he came to a riverbank, which he thought would be a good place to spend the winter, and so, he said, he built a house. Just like that. I'm sure it was a very simple house. But that's not necessarily bad.

These days many of us look back nostalgically on such hand-built houses, the product of one person's vision and labor. We want that kind of control over our own homes, with more comfortable conditions, of course. But even when you do build your own home, the control sometimes seems to slip away in the process of taking everyone's advice.

One problem with specialization is that arbitrary distinctions between jobs begin to be taken too seriously. I'm constantly meeting people who think that structuring a space and planning how it will work involves strictly practical decisions. And then, when that's done, you decorate the space, which is the aesthetic part of home design. But from first to last, functional and aesthetic considerations can't be separated. The dimensions of space and its structural materials determine the basis of its style. And what color you put in the walls, what furnishings you select, and so on, determine to a great degree how the space will function.

The way to maintain a single vision in a home is to make it your vision. Have the confidence that you can understand the implications of what dif-ferent specialists advise, and you can learn from them. But in the end you have to see it in your head. Not just the surfaces, but from the ground up, the entire environment. This kind of seeing is a skill that anyone can develop who's aware of his surroundings and has a normal visual imagination.

Most of my clients think making space plans is dull; the exciting part comes later. They haven't been exposed to the way different patterns in space affect its character. When I make a plan, in one part of my mind I'm thinking of the functional aspects of the plan, but simultaneously I'm picking up on the feeling of the space.

Approach a space plan as if it's a sketch or a painting. Treat it as work of art not a blueprint. It's very exciting when someone discovers the power of a drawing on paper to express different moods and realizes the freedom he or she has to create different kinds of environments.

There are some dry aspects to planning, of course. You do have to know the measurements of your space. You may be able to get plans from the architect who did your home or from the building managers. These should give you not only the dimensions but information on where structural columns are and what your electrical and heating arrangements are. At the lower right-hand corner there is a scale, for instance: $\frac{1}{8}''=1'\text{-}0''$ (which means that one-eighth of an inch on the drawing equals one foot of real space). For your purposes, a one-eighth-inch scale will probably be too small to work with comfortably. A quarter- or half-inch scale will probably be better. I usually work with a quarter-inch scale myself, unless the space is very large (then the eighth-inch scale may be better) or very small (a half-inch scale may be indicated). Bringing up the size of the drawing can be done by photo enlarger or by simply redrawing the plans yourself.

If you aren't fortunate enough to have an existing plan, you'll have to draw your own, and this is how to begin. Take a tape measure and, starting at one corner of the room, measure along the wall until you run into something, and then measure that. For example, if you come up to a fireplace, measure how far it projects into the room and how wide it is. The aim is to have a 3-D picture of the walls as well as an accurate record of their lengths and of the distances between windows, the width of doorways, and so on.

If you encounter an alcove with a curved wall, an easy way to measure it is to stand directly in the center of the opening of the alcove and measure the distance to the point at the center of the opposite wall. (If you're not sure you can find the center exactly enough, use a T bar to be sure you're running your tape at right angles to the alcove opening.) In most cases, if you know the distance to this point and the distance to the corners of the alcove opening, this is good enough for making your plan. Occasionally, you may want to measure additional points for greater accuracy, such as the points midway between the center and the corners. But if the curve of alcove is an exact semicircle, then all you need to know is the radius, and you can draw the curve to scale with a piece of string or a fifty-cent piece or some other round item with the right radius.

If you come to windows or doors with molding, measure *either* to the edge of the molding *or* to the opening of the space; be consistent, and make a note of which you've done. If *very* fine fits are contemplated, you may have to take both measurements.

I also always measure the adjacent spaces to the one I'm working on, because sometimes I want to use them, to open up a wall or to build an additional closet or a sleeping niche. And when I get down to making my sketches for the furniture, I like to see the adjacent space, and sometimes make rough drawings of what might be in there so I can get a sense of what it will be like to walk from one area to the other.

It may also be important to note electrical outlets and plumbing. Structural columns. Overhead light fixtures. Be sure to show the depth of any windows. There would be more window seats in this world—and they can be so pleasant!—if more people were aware of this space while making plans.

When I work, I draw up the scale plan on white paper with a pencil. I think, though, most people find it easier to use graph paper for this. Then I get out a *roll* of yellow tracing paper. In the art stores it's called "canary paper." With this paper you do what's called "overlays," that is, tracings of the dimensions of the space (you don't need to include every detail) on which you try out different furniture arrangements. Be extravagant when you buy the paper, and trace to your heart's content. The more drawings you make, the better. It may take twenty to thirty drawings before you loosen up and begin to get the feel of the shape of the space in relation to furniture. For the *entrance* of the Pump Room alone I did over two hundred drawings. Many more for the main part of the space.

The other supplies you should have at hand are No. 2 pencils, erasers, lots of imagination, and a couple of cocktails or jays to relax the brain. Put the tracing paper over the plan and start sketching.

I realize that in making space drawings I have an advantage over a beginner because I can draw to scale freehand almost any standard piece of furniture or standard reclining person. Most books advise that you make scale cutouts of any furniture you plan to use in the space, and then work with these pieces on your plan. I don't like this approach because it changes space design from a creative, subjective activity to puzzle-solving with rigid little pieces. Patterns in the space should evolve in your imagination. Later is the time to worry whether you can actually bring them into being. If you're working with a little rectangle for a dining room table, you'll never come up with an S shape or a diamond shape.

You may want to have scale drawings of pieces of furniture at hand for reference. But try to do your sketches freehand. After you've done a dozen or so, you'll find you can draw in the furniture spontaneously. Don't worry about inches accuracy until your final plan. On paper it doesn't cost anything to try out an idea.

I have to emphasize the point once more: When you make overlays and start sketching in your ideas, *this is the most important moment in the design process*. Working with ground plans is the *only* way to create an unusual, appealing, memorable space. You can't get the same result by pushing around pieces of furniture or eyeing a room. Doing the drawings is *the* secret of trade. The rest is frosting.

As you work, you'll begin to sense how different shapes in space evoke different feelings. Sharp right angles are severe. Acute angles jutting into the space are even more severe and unexpected and challenging. Rounded sinuous forms are organic and seductive. But circles may have a sophisticated cosmopolitan character. Large masses can produce a heavy, strong mood. Smaller shapes, widely dispersed, make for a light, open feeling.

Here are four plans for a small lounge, each with a different emotional impact. Drawing 1 has a conservative, organized, sedate feeling. Banquettes with pillows are placed along three walls. The coffee table is neatly, almost predictably in the most "important" corner, that is, the corner opposite the entrance. The banquette nearest the entrance has a rounded edge to avoid accidents involving shins and a sharp corner, and also to soften the squared-off character of this arrangement. There would be three pendant lights on runners, so that they could be adjusted for reading anywhere on the banquettes. Drawing 2 is bold and strong. The angles create an unexpected perspective that will make the space seem larger. The arrangement is weighted toward the right to draw people toward the main gathering areas. When the entrance to a room is in a corner, as this one is, the shapes should be arranged to draw one forward, to entice the person entering to explore the space. The banquettes with platforms behind them break the space into three levels, which not only provides more surface area for lounging but enhances the visual interest and encourages informality. The highest levels make good private places, or can be used as "tabletop" space. Drawing 3 is soft, sophisticated, and reminiscent of Art Deco. Formal but not rigid. The open space and curved shapes encourage both movement and relaxation. Drawing 4 is sinuous, organic, young, sexy. The narrow entrance to the small main seating area creates an intimate mood. (Incidentally, the platforms in these plans

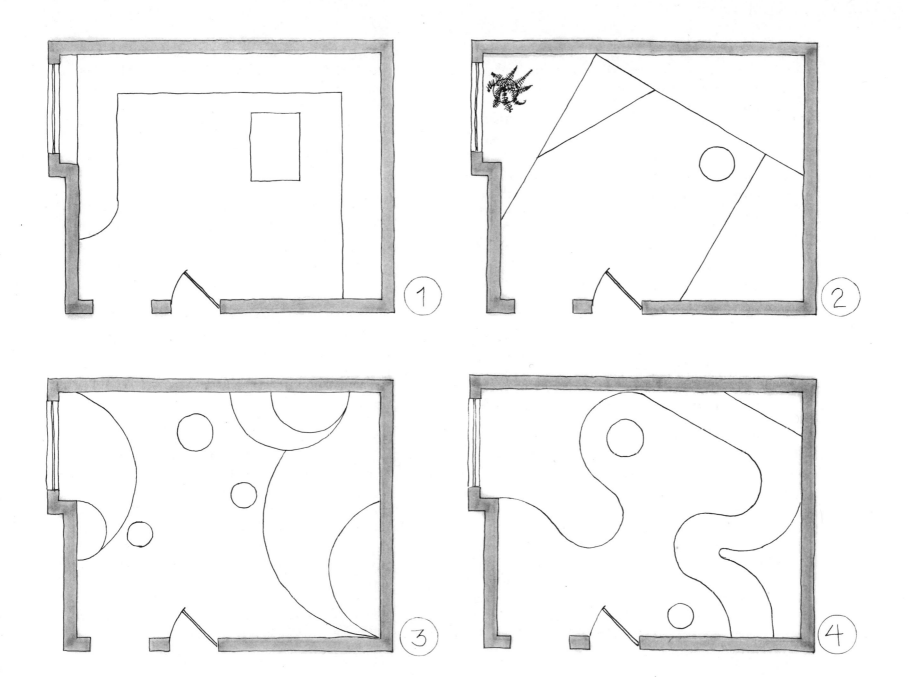

1

2

3

4

63

aren't elaborate or expensive. They're made of plywood covered with carpet. The banquettes are also simple, made of plywood, padded with polyurethane foam, and covered with fabric.)

As you do your drawings certain ideas will keep recurring. In this room, for example, multilevels seemed to work very well, because individual pieces of furniture would take up too much space and make the room feel cramped and formal. Once I started to think about different levels, I kept returning to the idea.

Don't give in immediately when an idea first appeals to you. If you sketch in, say, a window banquette or a circular arrangement of seating, try to get away from it. Plan something very different. If you find you're working with right angles, force yourself to work with curves, and vice versa. If you still keep coming back to a particular idea, if you can see vividly what the room will be like with it, if you begin to yearn to build the room that way, if any other arrangement just couldn't be as good—then you know it's right.

These are the most common mistakes people make in space planning: They worry over how to fill a space instead of how to create the possibility of movement and relaxation. They try to force pieces of furniture into a plan. (Ideally, I like to begin my drawings with few if any particular pieces of furniture in mind.) They're uptight and make static, symmetrical drawings, in which nothing's floating (except in front of a fireplace) and right angles dominate. Don't begin by worrying about what will fit. Instead, think about lines, movements, patterns, pictures; work with squares, circles, angles, blobs, diagonals, teardrops, spirals, and stars.

My students make similar mistakes, but they learn quickly and so can you. It's exciting when you understand that you can throw out the old ideas, create your own shapes, take off from the architecture instead of being trapped in it. You feel such a sense of elation and freedom, you think you'll never get bogged down again. Unfortunately you will. But not as badly.

Let's consider some of the structural shapes you may have to work with. Circular and oval spaces are lovely and extravagant and, today, rare. They leave too much unusable space and are too expensive. We're all programmed into right-angle living anyway.

Circular forms suggest wholeness and quiet, and are irresistably focused on the center. At least I feel that the magnetism of the center shouldn't be ignored or played off, unless, perhaps, the space is very large. The center is usually where I'd put the harp in a music room, the desk in an office, the bed in a bedroom.

A circle or oval is the ideal shape for a foyer. When a guest is greeted at the center of this space, he is figuratively at the center of the host's attention, the most important person in the home at that moment.

Ovals and circles are poor shapes for stimulating flow, mixing, give and take. The center is too strong. But centeredness can be an asset in a space that can be focused on one person or one group, such as an office (for example, the Oval Office), dining room, kitchen, study.

A large circle or oval is wonderful for dancing. Corners are totally unnecessary in a ballroom. (For square dances, though, rectangles are best.)

Alas, the days of the dramatic circular or oval

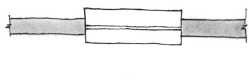

WINDOW

DOOR

On a floor plan, this is how a window is shown. And this is how a door is shown. Note, I indicate which way the doors open. Very important. For example, once, I drew a plan for a room with three doors. After I'd shown how they all opened, I could see there was no living space left.

foyer with marble floors and a grand staircase are gone with the wind. "Foyers" today are more apt to be long halls of the fun house type or eighteen inches of gloomy space in front of a blank wall. Step into a foyer, and you may find yourself walking into a corner or staring at the risers on a staircase. In such cases, it's sometimes as well to get rid of the foyer even if it means doing something strange, such as exposing a kitchen.

If you can't remove a wall that's in the way, do something special with it. Cover it in an unusual material or put up a good piece of art. In one instance, when the foyer (actually a hall) was so small I was sure guests were going to bump into the walls, I padded the walls with bumpers (twelve-inch strips of plywood, covered with two-inch-thick polyurethane foam and white linen). If guests can't see where they're supposed to go, lights can be used to direct them—a series of track lights, wall sconces, Christmas lights, or the like.

Square or almost square rooms can be problematic. A square is as centered as a circle but not as pleasing, more strong and rigid. Within a square, unless the space is very large, it's difficult to get away from strictly symmetrical patterns without creating a disturbing imbalance. But too much squareness imposes an uncomfortable awareness of four enclosing walls. Working with diagonals is one approach to weakening the impact of a square. Another approach is to introduce curving patterns.

Like a circular space, a square can be a good shape for a dining room or bedroom. It's ideal for a kitchen.

One of the questions I'm asked most often is what to do with a long, narrow room, or even an

Most rooms are
rectangular. The
right angles can be
accepted and
emphasized.

Or worked against
with the use of
diagonals.

entire long, narrow apartment, i.e., a railroad flat. Usually the answer is to interrupt the tunnel effect with lines running at right angles to the long walls. Verticals also tend to distract the eye from the length of the space. I don't like room dividers in this situation because they tend to make the space seem more cramped without adequately solving the problem; however, a platform banquette or bench extending partway across the space can be effective. Also, a rug or even a stripe running across the space can help; seating arranged on an angle or at right angles to the wall; square and round furniture and rugs, rather than rectangular shapes; mirrors on the long walls (but not the end wall, which would emphasize the length). Note that by not lining up the furniture along the walls, you allow for more pleasant seating as well as de-emphasizing the narrowness.

Actually, it's unfortunately quite common to see a well-proportioned rectangular room turned into a tunnel by poor furniture arrangement. For example, here's a (real) room with *two* sofas, *two* coffee tables, and *two* bookcases, all running lengthwise.

L-shaped entertainment and dining spaces have become common since the 1960s. The motive for building them isn't entirely a wish to create interesting, enjoyable rooms. The L shape gives an impression of spaciousness in apartments and houses that are getting smaller and smaller. But often the impression can't be translated into a reality. Many L-shaped rooms aren't suitable for more than six dining (if that) or six in the living room. (The L shape, however, can be excellent for a private or semi-private space used by one or two people, such as a bedroom, study, or den. Then, the foot of the L may be used for a desk area, a TV, or whatever.)

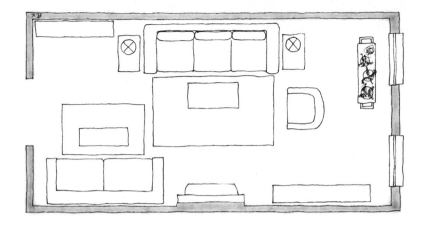

A TYPICAL POORLY PLANNED LIVING ROOM

69

A broad L like this ⌐ is quite a pleasant space. But a skinny L like this ⌐ isn't much better than two narrow rooms. To aggravate the problem, there are often entrances at opposite ends of the L, so you have to plan for traffic flow though the whole area. The temptation is to line up the furniture out of the way along the walls, but of course this isn't the most attractive arrangement.

In general, with L-shaped entertainment areas, I usually try to make an easy flow from one part of the space to the other, stressing their continuity rather than their separation. I maintain a single style of furnishing and often try to make the foot of the L resemble a lounging alcove rather than a dining room.

A more elegant variation of the L is the C or U shape, which is found most often in expensive homes, such as new co-op apartments. These are interesting shapes because the bottom of the C or U provides a strong natural focal point. The entrance may be here, with a dining area to one side and an entertainment area to the other. Or there might be a dining place in the center, with entertainment space in one wing and a private desk and study in the other. Again, the chief problem is to provide for traffic flow through the space.

A broad rectangular shape is attractive and functional for entertaining and gathering, and is the standard shape for living and dining rooms. Within a broad rectangle it's relatively easy to achieve balance without resorting to static symmetrical designs. You can throw weight in various directions. You needn't put the sofa in the center of one wall or float it exactly halfway the length of the room. You can put it at an angle across a corner, or at one end of the room, or float it almost anywhere.

If an entertainment space has a fireplace, this is usually made the focus of the main seating area. But don't turn a fireplace into an altar—especially if the climate is warm and the fireplace doesn't work anyway. In such a case, consider ignoring the fireplace. I worked on one such room where I put only a large ottoman in front of the fireplace, with the main seating unit at the end of the room near a window, balanced by a large Oriental folding screen in front of the entrance.

In a rectangular space that has no distinctive features, which is common in new apartment buildings, it's tempting to put a big sofa in the center of one wall and make this the focal point. A painting may be hung behind the sofa, not because this is the best place for viewing the painting, but to enhance the importance of this wall. More often than not, the effect is static, and the mediocrity of the sofa, not to say the art, is painfully emphasized.

More movement and variety can be brought into such a space by using smaller seating units. And if you have a good painting, you can show it better without a sofa in front of it.

There are times when one yearns for the charming, oddly shaped room. This is particularly true in some modern homes where the ceilings are low and the architecture banal. Alcoves and niches are treasured for providing relief from straight lines and making a space seem larger. In fact, one way to turn an ordinary room into an intriguing one is by building an alcove out from one side or by opening up one end with an alcove, like the apse of a church.

70

A contemporary treatment of a classic ceiling, in white gloss and beige, with two chocolate stripes.

Canted ceilings or even just ceilings of different heights break up the monotony of identical boxlike spaces. A low ceiling creates a sense of intimacy and warmth, whereas a high ceiling is dramatic, expansive, and formal. In a house that lacks any visually intriguing features, it sometimes helps to make a higher ceiling in one or two areas. Sometimes you can steal a couple of feet from a bedroom, den, or attic upstairs. Sometimes you can lower the entrance floor by stealing a couple of feet from the basement. I'm doing this just now in one part of an entrance floor in order to drop in a seating area. A similar but less complicated change is to put in skylights or expose beams. Ceilings with beams or interesting angles can be exploited, for example, by lighting them from below to emphasize the planes and shadows. A more complicated project is a domed ceiling, but it can be beautiful.

To compensate for low ceilings, it helps to stay with low, horizontal lines in the space. Large pieces of furniture and vertical lines make a claustrophobic effect.

An alternative approach to boxlike architecture is to break up the space with platforms (most conveniently made with plywood covered with carpet). Different floor levels are unexpected and often exciting. There's something of the child in us that makes a little climbing fun. Moreover, platforms can increase your useful space. By building platforms, or banquettes, on two levels around the edge of a room, you can have two lounging levels or a lounging and storage area. The traditional sofa against the wall is a more wasteful use of space. And the height of a platform gives it a sense of privacy a sofa lacks.

71

A platform can be used to stress a part of the space; for example, to identify a seating area, I might build it on a one-step or two-step platform. And a platform can transform a small dining space in a corner into something special, particularly if it makes possible a better view from a window.

A platform in the entrance of a room creates a dramatic feeling because as you come in you view the space from an unusual perspective. And it dramatizes the arrival of guests.

Sofas are formal, dictating a specific way and pattern of sitting. Platforms and banquettes encourage sitting or lying in whatever manner you like. But they're also seen as special, elegant, and more interesting than the usual furnishings. Platforms are particularly nice in modern apartments with windows that are hard to see out of.

When it's possible, I may work directly with windows themselves to create variety, for example, by building out an alcove with a bay window (which also creates additional seating space) or by building a window that slants away from the house toward the ground (like the old cellar doors), which is lovely when it rains. I sometimes put round windows in hallways, bathrooms, or children's rooms (because children love them).

In an apartment you can't ordinarily rebuild the windows, but sometimes you can rebuild doors or walls to get a slanting plane or a curved line for a change from the right angles. If you have a couple of feet of floor space to spare, you can rebuild walls to slant away as they rise, which helps keep paintings out of reach and harm. A doorway can be transformed by removing the door and rebuilding the sides in an A shape. As you've seen, I like to build out circular and triangular banquettes from the walls. Also to round off, or curve, the corners of rooms, and to build arched doorways.

To some extent, of course, these are playful changes, nice but not strictly necessary. The feelings they're intended to evoke—of energy, softness, complexity, fun, mystery—can be evoked in other ways, perhaps, without altering the architecture. But in certain kinds of mass-produced apartments and houses the need for architectural variety is terrific. I know people who are unhappy in apartments that are convenient and practical but just plain dull. And when they realize there are thousands and thousands of almost identical apartments all around them, they feel even worse. Playful changes may be frivolous but they're not meaningless.

THE BASICS: WALLS, FLOORS, AND CEILINGS

Shopping is fun. And after you buy the right clothes and cars, furniture and appliances, address and image, you'll end up living the good life. This message is delivered to us hundreds of times a day, beginning with the morning newspaper and ending with the late-night TV movies. It's created a fantastic consumer appetite. But still the good life always seems to be going on someplace else.

When people get hung up over what kind of clothes to buy or how to decorate their homes, they usually can't articulate what the problem is. I do know one young professional woman in Manhattan who left her apartment almost empty and said frankly she was afraid of "defining" herself. But this kind of insight is rare. More often a person who's feeling undefined grabs at the nearest ready-made definition. It's wiser to let things be for a while. There'll always be furniture in the stores.

Most manufacturers of furnishings and many home decorators are packaging life-styles along with products. That *Cosmopolitan* girl has a brass bed, at least one lover, and eats brunch instead of breakfast on Sunday. Nice suburban families practice physical fitness (sailing or tennis); paint the outsides of their houses white; and buy Early American, not Louis XV.

If you want to live in someone else's life-style, you can outfit your home from one of the model rooms in any good department store. And you'll get plenty of compliments. But you won't have an authentic home, your own home.

I meet many people who are straining to be original. They hire me because they want something different. But I'm the same Spiros wherever I am. What's different, and original, is the personality of each client. Your home will be unique when it's uniquely suited to you. Fixing it and furnishing it involves as much learning about yourself as learning about paint finishes or antiques' prices.

Don't let your home panic you into buying. Don't even be quick to take materials or furniture that's given you. A young couple I know is struggling to adapt their living room to a weird Victorian love seat that someone gave to them and that they don't even like that much.

If your home is empty, leave it that way for a while. Sit quietly in the middle of the floor and look around you. Try to become aware of what you like and don't like about the space, what's attractive and what's ugly. If your home is already furnished and "decorated," it's much more difficult to really see it. Start by giving away furniture or other objects you know you don't like. Make floor plans to help yourself be aware of the space itself instead of what's in it. Relax. Sit quietly. Focus on the basic architectural elements and the pattern of natural light.

Walls, Floors, Ceilings, Windows, Doors. These architectural elements create and define your space. What you might do to enhance or improve, alter or disguise them depends on their condition, the amount of money you want to spend, whether you're renting or own your own home, whether you plan to move in the near future, how well the character of the architecture suits your temperament, and so on. Above all, the space must be made to accommodate your needs. If you're a professional photographer, you need a darkroom. If there are two children in your family, each must have some privacy. So there are no absolute rules that can be applied. But the architecture of your home will provide you with certain definite problems and, if you're lucky, definite assets as well.

It's important to evaluate the architectural problems realistically. You may have the money and time to renovate much as you please, but there is a point when one is just throwing money out the window. When it seems to me that a client's plans aren't going to give good value, I usually try to go over each item, pointing out what the cost will be and discussing whether for the same money we could do something better.

Recently I've been working with a young couple in New Jersey who own a fairly small, three-bedroom home on quite a beautiful piece of land. Their original plans involved putting in skylights, exposing beams, removing some walls, stripping others down to brick, building a large fireplace (in a small living room), and so on. The cost for just the structural changes would have run to at least $15,000, but in the end they would still have had only a small (more charming but not distinguished) house. And they were expecting a baby, so space was certainly going to become important.

What this couple really wanted, when we talked about it, was a home that related better to the land around them, a home in which there was more light and more of a view, more use of natural materials, more of a feeling of country than suburbs. They also wanted, as most everyone does, more space for themselves (better organized, more luxurious space, of course), as well as a temporary nursery for the baby, without sacrificing room for guests.

The most elaborate and clever renovations still couldn't accomplish all this. I suggested that they start thinking of adding on rather than rebuilding. We're still doing a substantial amount of renovation, but we've also glassed in the runway from the house to the garage to make a combination breakfast room, plant room, and solarium. We've redone the garage as a living room with a sleeping balcony for guests. The fireplace they wanted is now here—a large one, made of local stone. In the main house, the old guest room has now been made part of the master bedroom.

It's easier to criticize someone else's plans than to evaluate your own, but here are three cautions for avoiding a wasteful, possibly disappointing approach.

1. Don't get involved in renovation or redecoration without knowing the full cost. Figure out what you want to spend on your home in the next year or so, and use that as the basis of your budget. It's not just that a spending limit will keep you from being led into deep water by hard-sell decorators or salespeople. Making a budget will also give you an idea of where you are in your life. You may decide you'd rather move than renovate. You may decide you'd rather have one good piece of furniture than several commonplace items.

2. Beware of expensive renovation that doesn't increase your useable space. You can turn a cottage into a little jewel, but it will still be a *little* jewel. If you can have more space for the same price, this might answer your needs better. It could also very well be a better investment.

3. Beware of extensive renovation that will change the character of your home completely. You may be buying more style than substance. A case in point involves a man I know in Louisiana whose house was badly damaged in a hurricane a few years

ago. It was a nice, big, unpretentious modern house. It's currently getting the plantation treatment: on the porch, fake eighteenth-century columns to replace the plain pillars; neoclassical trim inside; pseudotraditional wallpaper from New York; and so on. This is like going to the movies in evening dress.

Similarly, in New York these days any number of good old brownstones have had their insides removed and been modernized. But after all this surgery, they're still brownstones, except usually now with less rather than more living space. For the same money the owners could buy two or three brownstones. It's hard to see what the money's purchased, because it's all been spent on getting rid of things. And, more important, fashion will change, and there's a good chance that prospective buyers in the future will want walls just about where the old ones stood. (And believe it or not, people do make the mistake sometimes of removing structural walls and weakening their whole house. If you aren't an architect, don't be sure it can't happen to you.)

4. Finally, be cautious if you're undertaking major renovation because you're desperate and miserable and want to change your whole life. You may be chasing a fantasy that simply cannot be realized.

After years of practice, when I walk into a home I now see very quickly which elements in a space are disturbing (perhaps a low ceiling) and which are pleasing (a good view, a spacious doorway). But many people aren't fully conscious of what these features contribute to a room for better or worse.

You can sensitize yourself to the features that determine the character of a space by deliberately focusing on them in your own home and elsewhere. What kind of light flows into a space at different times of day? Is there a fireplace, a wall niche, a window, a view that's particularly pleasing? What are the problems? What don't you like? Structural beams on the ceiling? An obtrusive air conditioner? A dull floor? What is the feel, the aura of the space?

Every space does have a character. Character isn't limited to quaint settings. The character may not be altogether appealing. Maybe it's cold and arid. But you have to feel and understand it before you can cope with it.

Ideally, you should live with architecture that appeals to you. If you don't like English Tudor, don't move in and then disassemble the whole house. Stay away from styles you really can't stand.

If you're more or less compatible with your home, the first decision to make is whether to emphasize and enhance the architectural elements or whether to de-emphasize or even disguise them. In a well-built house or apartment (most often an old one) there may be good decorative detail, fine wood floors, marble fireplaces, and so on. If your budget allows, you'll probably want to enhance and draw attention to these features.

On the other hand, you may be faced with low ceilings and exposed pipes, small, undistinguished doors and windows, cramped rooms and hallways, and plaster falling down in chunks.

Enhancing architectural features essentially involves repairing, cleaning, and perfecting them. If they're very fine, they can be treated with a finish or color particularly chosen to attract the eye. And then display these features, don't obscure them. Don't hang drapes in front of elegant moldings or put large expanses of carpet over beautiful parquet floors.

Unfortunately, you may not always be able to repair to perfection. Theoretically, anything can be restored, but in actuality, it may be too expensive and impractical. If a ceiling or wall is stained, pitted, cracked, peeling, irregular, or otherwise in bad shape, try to find out its recent history before going to work on it. You may discover it was repaired and repainted not so long ago. Vibration from traffic, recurring dampness, and other chronic problems can be hard to cure. Get a diagnosis of the difficulty and an estimate of the cost of repair from two or three contractors that you've worked with before or your friends have used. Ask around. Good ones are hard to find.

In some cases it may be best to compromise and take a shortcut. Putting up sheet rock might be cheating, but you also have to get on with life.

Let's begin, though, with the floors, which are usually the most maltreated surface in a home. They're also your most important surface—first, because they represent the total space you have to live on, at least in terms of square feet. Second, floors give definite tone to a room. The color and texture of a floor, whether natural or painted wood, tile, or marble, suggests a particular mood and style, sometimes so strongly that if you don't want that mood, you may have to change the floor. Finally, floors affect two senses at once: sight *and* touch. There's not only a different look to a room with a polished wood floor, a carpeted floor, a linoleum floor, there's a different feeling to walking in it. If you're sensitive to sensual experience, you'll appreciate having different flooring materials in different areas for aesthetic as well as practical reasons.

Incidentally, there seems to be a personality factor in the selection of floor materials. I've noticed that people who like hard, highly polished surfaces tend to be active, quick, restless. Those who like many rugs or carpeting tend to be slower, quieter, gentler. But the ideal, I believe, is a balanced variety of surfaces, corresponding to different moods.

I almost always recommend repairing and displaying good wood floors. Clean, shining wood is a luxurious texture. The hardwoods (walnut, oak, beech, hazel, maple) are best for floors. Soft woods, such as red spruce and white pine, are attractive to look at but splinter and warp easily and require more care. Parquet tiles are popular (because they're not expensive and they're easy to install); they're also very nice. If you're lucky enough to have a floor of special quality, such as marquetry or the random-width flooring of the Colonial period, I imagine you're aware of its value and are taking good care of it.

If a floor has been well maintained and regularly waxed, then I like to stay with a wax finish. Over time a waxed floor develops a good patina. But I don't have to live with your floor or maintain it. If you aren't going to do the waxing, or you're going to resent and hate it, you can use polyurethane, which gives a sealed finish that protects the wood from stains and scratches for many years (under ordinary use).

In putting down polyurethane, it's important to have enough coats so that the floor is completely sealed. Two are usually recommended; but I usually use at least three. The finish should be even, with a clean shine all over. Dull spots (more common when the floor is uneven) mean that another coat is needed.

Polyurethane is advertised as giving a clear finish, but I've found that it almost always yellows the wood at least a little. This is not necessarily undesirable, but you should be aware of it. Lacquer will give you a clear finish, but it's harder to work with and not as durable.

Polyurethane comes in high-gloss, medium, and satin finishes. The high gloss creates a sparkle that will draw attention to the floor. The satin finish is still lustrous, but the floor will look softer, less crisp.

This leads us to a general principle: The more reflective the surface, whether because of finish or color, the more it will attract the eye. It's commonly believed that shiny surfaces make a space look larger, but in fact they can make it look smaller, because they emphasize the limits of the space. I think the reason so many people have the opposite idea is that a clean, bright look is often associated with an uncluttered, sparsely furnished space. But it's the absence of complications that makes the space look larger, not the shiny surfaces.

If you sand and stain the floors yourself, then of course you can control the color. And there are some beautiful and unusual stains, which can be used to striking effect. But first a word of warning. Handling those sanding machines isn't quite as easy as you may have heard. They weigh a couple of tons, and the sandpaper discs rip extremely easily, especially when a beginner is working with them. If you can get a pro to come in and do the job, you can save yourself a bad time. If you want to do the job yourself, get complete instructions from the renter of the machine, and look at a home handyman's book as well. The room will have to be emptied (sawdust gets in everywhere); loose boards and protruding nails have to be hammered down; you'll need two sanders (a small one for corners and closets) and about twice as many sandpapers as will be recommended. Be sure you know how to run the machines

A rough wood floor, brightened with a polyurethane finish, is the dominant texture in this space.

without making too many gouges, and how to cope with edges and corners. Explain the kind of floor you have, how bad its condition is, and what kind of finish you want to use on it (the glossier the finish, the smoother the surface should be). The dealer should tell you not only how to operate the machines but how many passes your floor will probably require.

Staining is another job I prefer to leave to a pro. Getting the stain on evenly is tricky, and mistakes are hard to correct.

The most popular colors for wood floors are natural oak and a medium walnut stain. Both are decoratively safe; being neither strikingly light nor dark, they won't as a rule interfere with whatever else you want to do with the area. Their effect is informal, easygoing.

The darker the wood, the more formal and sophisticated the effect. A deep, rich stain (you can go as far as ebony) is more work to maintain (dirt, scratches, and scuffs show readily), but the result is very impressive in a heavy, lush way.

At the other extreme you can have a floor bleached or "pickled." This is expensive and, again, not very practical if you have to worry about maintenance. The floor doesn't stand up well to traffic, but the effect is light and delicate. A polyurethane finish will make it tougher and can be scrubbed down if need be.

I made a mistake once by bleaching the floor in a small extra room in a family home. This room was hardly ever used, and I thought I'd make it into a pretty, light, mostly white parlor. I didn't worry about the upkeep. But once the room was done, it was so charming that everyone started using it, and the floor couldn't take the traffic. I had to redo it.

You should pick a stain as carefully as you would color for a wall. Mahogany gives a red tone; walnut, brown tones; cherry is red-orange; and so on. If in doubt, stay with a medium shade. You don't want to get overcommitted to a color while you're still working on the floors; this can cut way back on your choices later.

The texture and polish of a fine wood floor can be enhanced by lighting, for example, by focused down light from the ceiling or by light along the baseboards. Baseboard light is also a good way of lighting passages, for example, from bedroom to bathroom. It saves electricity and is visually pleasing.

A wood floor is also enhanced by contrast with nonwood furnishings, that is, in juxtaposition with fabric, stainless steel, chrome, brass, glass, plastic, and so on. Reflective materials augment each other, so that when, for example, polished metal and polished wood are together, each reflects the other, and both become secondary sources of light. This kind of effect can be exciting, but, overdone, it becomes glaring and harsh. What's "too" harsh is really a personal judgment, but if you take one step at a time, you'll be able to control the final effect. If you end up squinting because of the glitter, you've gone too far.

Rugs and wood floors also complement each other, of course. But only put down a rug because you like the look and feel of it, not because you think you should cover the floor with something. Don't put down more rugs than you need or a larger rug than you need. Rugs or mats are desirable wherever you may be stepping with bare feet (beside a bed, in a bathroom) or resting your feet (in front of a lounging area) or sitting on the floor (in front of fireplace). You also need some kind of cushioning where you walk and stand constantly (in a workroom, for example, or a kitchen). Cushioned vinyl is often used in these service areas, but indoor–outdoor carpeting is also practical when the danger of soiling isn't too severe.

Often people who need a three-by-six rug for comfort in a bedroom go out and buy a nine-by-twelve carpet just out of habit. Most of the material they've paid for is hidden under the bed, neither used nor seen.

Whenever there's a choice between a carpet and a rug, I almost always prefer a rug, because there's a wonderful variety of interesting rugs available, whereas carpeting tends to be dull. And rugs are more flexible. You can change them around for a different effect or to be sure they aren't worn unevenly. In this way a good rug can last a lifetime or more. But a carpet, especially a wall-to-wall one, can't be moved around easily, if at all, and therefore almost always wears out prematurely. If you move, you can always take rugs with you. Besides, rugs are easy to clean. There's nothing wrong with the old-fashioned method of hanging them on a line and beating out the dust.

I have a lot of arguments with clients over my aversion to wall-to-wall carpets. In almost every home there are a number of status symbols, which really aren't all that useful or wonderful but which have been promoted to the point that people think they can't live without them. The dining room set is one example. Wall-to-wall carpeting is another. I've heard of many people on tight budgets putting down hundreds of dollars worth of carpeting before even buying a comfortable chair to sit on. I know a house in Connecticut that has beautiful hand-laid oak floors in the living and dining rooms. When

it was sold recently, the new owners, a lawyer and his wife, wanted to get in wall-to-wall carpeting as soon as possible, supposedly so that no one would slip on the wood and sue them.

I hear many arguments in favor of carpets, some good, some not so good.

1. Wall-to-wall carpeting increases the value of a home. Sometimes maybe yes, but most often I hear the other side. The new owners don't like the carpet, certainly don't want to pay for it or even to pay for having it removed. They just want it out. As a matter of fact, I can't think of a single case where the new owner liked the carpets to the point of saying they're what he would have chosen himself.

2. Carpets are easier to clean than wood floors and don't need to be cleaned so often. Actually carpets love pins, insects, stains, staples, particles of glass, fingernail clippings, and plain old dirt. Vacuuming doesn't totally clean them. If there seems to be less dirt when you have a carpet, it's not because the carpet is magically keeping away the dirt. It's because the dirt is in the carpet.

3. Carpeting is needed for insulation from drafts and noise. This is sometimes true. If insulation is badly needed, you might even carpet the walls and ceiling.

4. Carpeting is needed for cushioning, especially if the floor is very hard (cement, for example) or small children will be playing on it. This is sometimes true. I've lived with a cement floor and know how painful it can be to the feet. It should certainly be covered with something. A carpet should be considered along with cushioned vinyl or, if you can afford it, rubber or cork.

A wall-to-wall carpet is in some ways good in a child's room. All children spend a lot of time on

81

the floor. But carpet also has drawbacks in a child's room. Parents worry about damage, which is no fun for the child. And a carpet can interfere with certain kinds of play, such as setting up toy soldiers, running windup toys, building erector constructions. Probably the best kind of carpeting for a child's room is indoor–outdoor carpet with a fairly hard, smooth surface. Another possibility is to use a couple of rugs and leave the rest of the floor simple and easy to clean—covered with linoleum, a polyurethane finish, or the like.

Sometimes using a carpet as a cushion becomes ridiculous. If the carpet is so deep it's hard to walk through, you've gone too far. I've even heard of people with this kind of carpet putting down plastic runners for guests to walk on. I worked on a large mansion in Miami Beach that had a carpet with such a thick design that you had to walk around it. The height of the pile on the design must have been an additional three inches above an already two-inch basic pile. I understand it cost more than $100 per square yard. As you can guess, I had nothing to do with it—it came with the house!

5. Carpet is necessary to prevent people slipping and falling. I agree that this can be important on stairs and sometimes in halls, although a runner is just as useful and less expensive than wall-to-wall installation. And check from time to time that the carpet or runner on the stairs isn't loosening up. If it doesn't fit snugly, it's more dangerous than nothing at all.

6. Carpeting is the best means of covering a floor in poor condition. Not necessarily. I often recommend painting a poor floor. And paint is relatively cheap. You can repaint a floor a different color anytime without feeling guilty, but tearing up a wall-to-wall carpet is like burning money. Most people can't bring themselves to do it no matter what.

7. Carpet is most useful for protecting wood floors for the enjoyment of the next tenants. Correct.

Shopping for rugs and carpets can be confusing, because of the number of trade names for synthetic fibers and the wide variations in quality. Unless you're an expert or have one along, stay away from cut-rate bargains. Shop at a reputable store.

The quality of a carpet depends not just on the fiber used but also on its ply, the type of weave, and the backing. The material will not wear well unless the surface yarns are closely woven. To check pile density, bend back a part of the carpet: The backing should not show through.

If you're spending a significant amount of money on a rug or carpet, it's important to research the type you need and what's your best buy. There are virtually no guarantees if the carpet wears out on you or fades or doesn't clean well. Most carpet manufacturers provide booklets with carpet information. Consumer's Union does a good job of testing different brands. And if you still don't have the information you need, you can ask the Carpet and Rug Industry Institute for help (Box 1568, Dalton, Georgia 30720). The factors you should consider and rate are durability, ease of cleaning, resistance to crushing, resistance to fading.

For wall-to-walls, use a professional installer, or you'll surely be disappointed. To maintain the carpet, be sure you know how to clean up spots. (A detergent cleaner can be made with one teaspoon neutral detergent, one teaspoon white vinegar, one quart warm water.) Get the dealer's advice on how and how often the carpet should be cleaned. Note that, as with wood floors, the very light and very dark colors show dirt the most. Carpets of a medium color are best for areas of heavy traffic.

If you decide to paint a floor instead of carpeting it, consider taking full advantage of the color and life paint can bring to a space. Too often people paint a floor brown or beige, the typical colors of wood or conservative carpeting. But a painted surface doesn't have the sheen of polished wood or the texture of a carpet to compensate for a dull color. In addition to brown and beige, there are deck paints in several shades of gray that are not only boring but unpleasantly cold.

Paint is usually chosen because the floor is poor, and therefore, it should really brighten and freshen. Avoid the muddy and dull colors. It may not be practical to use a light shade, but at least try to use a bright one. I have a wood floor in my bathroom I painted white with several coats. In our loft building, we've also painted the hall floors bright colors: yellow on the ground floor, then orange and red. Polyurethane paints for floors come in an excellent selection of colors, and they are simple to care for.

Working with paint you're free to experiment with your own designs. For a border or overall pattern that's too complicated to do by hand (such as a flower pattern, perhaps) you can cut your own stencils or buy ready-made ones. You can spatter a floor with flecks of two or three different colors, a type of decoration that was popular in Colonial days. This gives a feeling of texture and warmth to the surface, and the effect is cheerful and informal. Stripes, such as racing stripes, are amusing and can be used to accentuate or de-emphasize architectural features.

A floral design stencilled on the floor.

For example, a stripe across the floor of a long, narrow space stops the eye and distracts from the narrowness. A stripe or stripes on the diagonal in a small room can make it seem larger by setting up an unexpected perspective.

Painting a floor a bright color can, of course, be risky, because the color tends to define the space and limit what you can do with it thereafter. But there's not much to worry about if you're painting a small or informal area—kitchen, hall, workroom. And babies respond to bright colors, not the faded pastels, the powdery pinks and blues of traditional nurseries.

For surfaces that will get tough wear I most often use the popular vinyl asbestos tiles or indoor-outdoor carpeting. Pirelli rubber tiles (from Italy) make a handsome floor that's kind to the feet. They're expensive and the selection is limited, but in some spaces they're very good. Linoleum is also worth a look now. It's available in more attractive colors and patterns than in the past, and some types stand up quite well to hard use.

Synthetic floor coverings needn't be limited to service areas or children's rooms. I've used vinyl tiles as a border in some very elegant rooms. The choice shouldn't be based on old ideas of what goes where, but on what kind of surface you like to live with and what kind of maintenance you're prepared to do.

Before buying synthetic flooring, take the same precautions as when buying carpet. Go to a reputable dealer and explain what kind of use the floor will get. Be sure you understand the qualities of the different types available, and check and rate brands for durability, resilience, flexibility, cushioning, stain resistance, and so on. Two good brands may differ greatly in their best features; for example, one may be resilient and right for a floor on which you'll put heavy furniture, another might be poor in that respect but well cushioned.

Have the flooring professionally installed if this is recommended. If you're installing it yourself, be sure the material will work on your floor surface. If the floor is uneven; it will have to be smoothed, usually by a covering of plywood.

Floors of marble, slate, clay, ceramic, or brick are almost always a joy, at least to someone like me who loves a clean surface and natural materials. But they're very expensive. And they're also cold and hard underfoot, which is some consolation if you can't afford them.

A floor should be beautiful, but deciding how much emphasis to give it may take some thought. It can be a mistake to accent a floor too sharply, even with a fine patterned rug. For example, a friend of mine has a large foyer covered in black and white tiles. The foyer is between the living room and the dining room and can be seen from both. It's a visual nuisance. It jumps out at you, and quieter colors and patterns can't compete with it. It pays to think in terms of space rather than rooms. If my friend had treated these two rooms and the foyer as a single space, she wouldn't have made this mistake.

A problem I constantly encounter is the prized Oriental rug in jumpy colors. The owner won't give it up, even though the rug brings into the space all the color and pattern the eye can tolerate. So what else can you put there? In the regions where these rugs were created, homes weren't full of so many other objects and fabrics.

84

There's a limit to the amount of excitement you can generate in a space without causing malaise. If you want to feature other textures and patterns in the space, keep the floor simple. On a floor, subtle variations from the norm are enough to affect the mood. For example, I've been working on a family den where I've put down pine flooring on a diagonal, extending out onto an adjacent porch and up one wall as paneling. The room is easygoing and casual, but the unusual line makes it just a bit more elegant than most dens. In a child's room, I've painted small flowers on the floor. This is quieter than floral wallpaper but still establishes the room as pretty and feminine. And it leaves the walls free for the girl to use as she chooses.

In the past, walls have often been regarded as surfaces to be decorated—with murals, Oriental silk panels, wallpaper, and so on. In this century, we've been more interested in emphasizing the architectural character of the wall: its inherent shape, strength, texture, and relationship to the total structure and space. A decorated wall often seems fussy to us. Also, because we're so mobile and don't expect to live in the same place for a lifetime, we don't want to invest in murals or carving that makes the wall itself a work of art. We put art *on* the wall. In this sense, perhaps prehistoric men were more settled and stable than we are. They painted on the walls of their caves.

If you have good walls, you're lucky. Probably the best thing you can do is perfect them. Really good walls are rare and a great asset. They don't need decoration. Treated simply, painted a light, neutral tone, they'll allow you maximum flexibility in how you use the space. And plain walls can make

a space seem larger. Once you've covered them with wallpaper or fancy paneling, they become important, heavy features in the space. And constrict it.

However, as I said, check carefully into the practicality of repairing plaster walls that are in bad shape. If necessary, you can cover up a bad wall or ceiling with sheet rock, which will give you much the same appearance as plaster for less money. I do try to use plaster wherever possible, because it's superior in strength, insulating ability, and flame resistance. And skilled plastering is almost a lost art. But don't spend more than you feel you can afford on what may be intangible benefits.

Another solution to a bad plaster wall may be to go down to brick, if brick is underneath. But prepare for living with plaster dust for a while.

Basically, there are two types of finish for a wall: structural and applied. Structural finishes can be considered part of the wall itself: brick, stone, wood, stucco, plaster, and paint, etc. Applied finishes are put onto a wall and include wallpaper, fabric, cork, murals, etc. Generally, structural finishes are more neutral, less decorative than applied finishes, but there are numerous exceptions.

Defects in walls (waves, pits, bumps, and bulges) can be minimized by using a flat paint in a neutral or pale color—off-white, beige, taupe, gray, blue-gray, pale green, or pink. A high-gloss paint or a bright color will point up any blemish. On the other hand, a high gloss flatters a good wall, brightens a room, and is easy to clean. I most often use it in kitchens, bathrooms, hallways (especially when children are about), and on woodwork and trim that's in good condition. For most people, high-gloss walls are too sharp for a space that's going to be used

85

quietly. A high gloss can also be too bright in a room that gets good sunlight and is used regularly during the day. This is a personal matter. Some people's eyes are bothered by brightness and contrast in a room that to others is only pleasantly light.

Medium-gloss paint is a compromise solution, and often very nice. I sometimes use it when I might prefer high gloss but the walls aren't good enough; or to bring a fresh feeling into a room, especially one that's used during the day. It's a good choice in a home with children, because it cleans fairly easily.

If you're fortunate enough to have fine moldings, niches, pediments, and other decorative details you'd like to emphasize, an old solution and still a good one is to paint the wall and ceiling with a flat finish and do the trim with a gloss finish, usually in white. If you'd like to draw attention to a good, high ceiling as well, you can paint the molding at the top of the wall a contrasting color (the French used to use gold leaf).

City people see so many plain plaster walls that they tend to undervalue them and to overvalue other materials like brick, wood, stone, and stucco. It can be a selling point for an apartment to have a brick wall, even if the tenant has to tear through the plaster himself to get to it. Sometimes the brick turns out to be ordinary or actually ugly. There's brick and then there's brick. And even good brick can be too dark and heavy in some circumstances. Personally, I do like brick for its texture and warmth, but this doesn't mean it's always an improvement over plaster. Nor does it have to be treated with reverence. If the brick seems gloomy and rough, it can be brightened with paint, which will also minimize stains, rough spots, and other irregularities. In my own home, I've put a high-gloss white on brick, and the wall is not only bright and cheerful, it picks up and reflects changing shadows, light, and colors.

Wood paneling was originally an elegant and expensive means of insulation. The best work was custom-made for the room, with intricate moldings, inlaid panels, and decorative framing for the windows and doors. Today, even much simpler wood paneling is extremely expensive. It's almost invariably book-match veneer (on plywood), available in a wide range of woods, including teak, zebra wood, and walnut. There's usually little if any decorative detail. It's a favorite of big corporations and banks, who presumably can afford it and want to give an impression of permanence and vaguely English venerability.

In the 1950s, random-width pine paneling was popular, especially for suburban homes, in dens, playrooms, and bars. It was admired for its rustic, warm effect. But too much wood can be stark and monotonous. I've been in rooms that were supposed to resemble some kind of cozy ski lodge, with wood floor, paneled walls, and wood ceilings. It's like being shut up in a box. In the past, the monotony of wood was sometimes avoided by painting it—paneling, trim, doors, furniture. Today, we pay to have the paint stripped off. I don't like to see beautiful wood painted over, but there's nothing wrong with painting ordinary wood, in fact the effect can be very pleasing.

Personally, I dislike wood paneling, perhaps because of the kinds of homes that featured it when I was growing up. To me, it seems pretentious and heavy. I like more light and color. However, any kind of genuine paneling is better than the imitation

An inexpensive, curious wall or partition can be built out of linoleum and two-by-fours.

paneling that's been creeping into more and more homes as the price of wood rises. This phony paneling may be plywood with a sort of photograph of wood printed on the surface. Or it may be molded plastic. There are funny little indentations where the "planks" meet, and equally fake grain, knotholes, and wormholes. This kind of paneling is awful to touch.

If you like wood, don't settle for a photograph. In general, imitations of natural materials are unsatisfactory. I've been in homes that are very disconcerting, because the brick floor is linoleum, the marble counters are formica, the antique sideboard is plastic, and the fruit on top of it is wax. One's afraid to go to the john.

A good imitation can be clever and even beautiful in its own right. (And then it's often more expensive than the original.) But, most of the time imitations are disappointing. I always feel cheated when I go to look at a plant and it's plastic. How much would it cost to have a real plant instead?

In many homes that have been "decorated," the main thing that's been done is to put wallpaper on all the walls. In addition, it may be on cabinets, wastepaper baskets, and any other place one can stick it. Like wall-to-wall carpeting, wallpaper has been oversold. When a couple buys their first home, one of the first things they traditionally do is put up wallpaper. It's almost un-American not to.

But wallpaper should be used carefully, if at all, *especially* in a first home. If you aren't sure exactly how your home and your life in it will evolve, wallpaper can cause more problems than it's worth. Wallpaper usually imposes a highly defined character on a space. If the paper is gay and dainty, it's going to be hard to listen to Beethoven or read the news in that room. If it's somber and formal, it's going to be depressing on a spring day.

Wallpaper is designed to go with popular furniture and fabric lines and to sell to a large market. It's not art and all too often it's not even attractive decoration. You'd think twice about buying a painting that covered an entire wall. Wallpaper deserves just as much thought.

Wallpaper is really a problem when little children are around, as it's entertaining to peel. Even though it's not ideal for crayoning on, it will do on a rainy day.

Wallpaper can be nice in out-of-the-way places that tend to be dreary and neglected. A back hall, a laundry room, a pantry, a closet, in cabinets and on shelves. I don't think it's such a good choice for guest rooms, although here many people invest heavily in frilly, flowery paper, matching curtains and bedspreads, and so on. The idea is to make a fun little room to visit, even if you wouldn't want to live there. But it isn't fun to visit a frilly room if you hate frills.

Watch out for the kind of decorator who comes into your home and begins by selecting wallpaper. What you're apt to end up with is a virtuoso performance by the decorator that's disturbing and expensive.

When I first graduated from design school, I went to work for a successful decorator in Philadelphia. I lasted about three weeks. We worked according to formulas; for example, first we would pick a paper for the living room with at least three colors, and then these colors would provide the color scheme for the living room, dining room, and foyer. To be sure I understood, I was taken to a townhouse where we had work in progress. The paper in the living room was already up: a large, bold damask print. The colors were bright yellow, red, and green.

With this much color on the wall, you have only two choices: Either everything else in the space has to be kept neutral or you match the colors pretty carefully. The second approach can be tricky and costly, but it's the one this decorator always took. In this case, I remember we ordered a rug custom-made in Puerto Rico that incorporated the colors and design motif of the paper. It cost about $4,000. There were two Oriental lamps, and we "had" to redye the bases to get a matching yellow. It took three tries to get it right. Cost: $700. And so on.

Working this way, you make money on each item to be made, bought, or dyed. And once the client is committed to a complicated pattern and difficult colors, he isn't likely to fire you. Then what would he do? But just as important, I think, when the job's done, everyone can see how hard it was to pull off. ("Where did you *ever* get a rug to match that fabulous wallpaper?" "Oh, my decorator had it custom-made in Puerto Rico.")

I have to admit there have been some improvements in wallpaper. Vinyl "paper" cleans up easily and is particularly useful when there are little ones racing around. It comes in a good variety of colors and textures (such as a weave) and in several finishes from flat to glossy. In places that are really hard to clean, say around a stove, a good surface is ceramic tile. I know lots of people who'd like to do whole rooms in tile, but it's pretty expensive.

There's also a fairly wide selection of Japanese

grass papers on the market which have an element of texture that's lacking in traditional papers, and somewhat unusual colors.

By the way, don't try to use contact paper in place of wallpaper. A friend of mine wanted to brighten up a large old bathroom and started by putting some contact paper on the shelves. Then she thought it would look nice on one wall, so she went out and bought some more. Then having just one wall covered looked funny to her, so out she went for more again. After putting in much more work than she'd intended, she had a bathroom completely covered in contact paper that cost $300! This illustrates the advantage of thinking ahead and figuring costs.

An alternative to decorating with wallpaper is to use stencils. You can buy ready-made stencil patterns, but I like to design my own. You can buy all the materials at an art supply store. Ask for advice on how to proceed. (Beginners often make the pattern elements too small.) Start with a simple pattern. And consider covering only a small area, say, a border around the top of a wall or the inside of an alcove. You can always extend it if you want. Practice on drawing paper or cardboard before working on the wall, floor, or whatever. Most errors result from cutting the pattern with a blade that isn't sharp enough, or working with a brush that's too wet, or not taping the stencil on securely, or sweeping on the paint instead of using a more cautious jabbing motion, or sweeping the paint under the edges of the stencil instead of working from the edges toward the middle.

Fabric is a good, versatile way to cover a wall.

A textured wall is luxurious, and fabric provides somewhat more insulation than plain paint or paper. Usually it's a suitable cover for a poor wall, but a thin fabric should have a smooth wall underneath.

Fabric tends to draw attention to a wall, giving it weight. Often fabric on one wall is enough; on four walls the effect may be too strong.

Good, moderately priced fabrics for walls include burlap, which can also be painted over if you like; linen, which is lighter and finer in texture and comes in many colors and patterns; cotton, which is still lighter; polished cotton, which is bright and airy and comes in many decorative patterns; felt and flannel, which come in almost any solid color and have a very pleasant intimate feeling that's also somewhat serious—these materials are better for a den than a plant room, a man's bedroom rather than a young girl's room.

For extra insulation and a wall that's nice to be up against, pad the wall first with polyester, and then apply the fabric. Another possibility is to use lightweight carpet, and there are now square modules available that are easy to install.

There's no need to treat all walls in a space the same way. Walls can be painted different colors, or you can combine paint and fabric and paper, paneling and fabric or whatever. Accenting a wall with color, pattern, or texture can create visual interest in a dull space or emphasize a good architectural feature. It will also make the wall more important, distracting from a problem elsewhere, or balance an opposing weight (a large bookcase, for example).

Some practical points:

Mixing the finishes on walls should enhance

89

A clear, simple foyer—a mirror to one side for light and interest.

the utility of the space. For example, an alcove with a dressing table usually should have white or light-colored walls for more total light. In a living room or den, a corner for children might have vinyl walls.

The treatment of walls can be used to minimize problem features. A strong color and/or a heavy fabric (felt, burlap, or the like) can, as I've said, balance a heavy element in the space, such as a large sofa or a bookcase. In a long rectangular space, a strong reflecting color on the end walls will cut off the tunnel effect. And a bright wall can be used to draw attention away from an eyesore, such as bulky kitchen cabinets.

The use of mirrors on walls is a traditional idea that's very popular today. A mirror can increase the light in a space and make it look larger. Unfortunately it's often done poorly. A common mistake is to mirror an entire wall. Not many people like to see themselves constantly reflected in a mirror—some do, but not many. In one home I visit, there's a mirrored wall next to a sofa. When you sit there, you always have the feeling someone's watching you. During the course of an evening that mirror can get to be quite annoying.

Similarly, although a mirror along the side of a hallway can be nice, a mirror that reflects you coming in the front door can be an unpleasant shock.

Since the main thing a mirror does is reflect, try to use it where there's something worth reflecting: a sculpture, a window, a fireplace. A mirror at the top or foot of steps can be interesting, for you appear in it gradually. A mirror behind a table holding flowers, bric-a-brac, or the like is conventional. For a similar effect, you may be able to place a mirror at a right angle to one end of the table. A mirror at a right angle to a window wall creates an illusion of open space and lightens the room.

The best way to decide where to put a mirror is to take one off a closet door, or borrow one, and put it up in different places. If the effect is harsh you might want to try using tinted or smoked glass. I often recommend these to give an illusion of depth without the confusion of a double image. Bronze and solar gray are fairly widely available. Special shades, such as cobalt blue, can be had on special order. If you buy smoked glass, stay away from the kind with the fake veins that are supposed to make the mirror look antique.

Mirror glass can be bought or cut by a glazier in a variety of shapes. Round mirrors, framed and unframed, are common and work well in places like stair landings where the clarity of the image isn't very important. Working with squares, rectangles, diamonds, half-moons, etc., you can make any number of geometrical designs. For example, a hallway might be mirrored in a zigzag or striped pattern.

An unusual and handsome way to finish a wall is with nonreflecting tinted or colored glass. This is expensive and has to be professionally installed; your only saving would be that the wall underneath can be in poor condition. Plastic will give much the same effect, and is lighter and tougher. Generally, the atmosphere that this kind of finish evokes is formal (but not stodgy), sophisticated, and futuristic. Actually, I feel that tinted translucent plastic and glass will come to be used much more for interior walls. These are similar to rice paper, which conveys light while providing privacy. In homes and offices often the interior spaces, especially hallways, are poorly lit; sometimes one side of a home is always in shadow. Translucent walls can bring a soft light into otherwise gloomy spaces.

I often use translucent materials as interior partitions. Acrylic (Plexiglas) panels are available in translucent and opaque styles and in a number of colors (bronze, grays, blues, and even some pastels). The standard size is eight feet high and four feet wide, but they can be specially ordered in different sizes, the most common being ten by five and five by six. The panels can be set in aluminum frames on the ceiling and floor or simply hung from the ceiling. Even a single panel in front of a child's bed can create a needed degree of privacy. These panels are also excellent for creating pockets in front of an entrance to block off draughts—you've seen this arrangement in restaurants.

Another translucent material (also opaque) for partitions is stretch fabric. It can be attached to floor and ceiling with simple curtain rods. My bedroom "walls" are made of this material—attached with my favorite tool—the staple gun.

The main (nonstructural) function of a ceiling is to reflect light, which is why most people paint a ceiling white. And so do I most of the time. For the average, rather low, undecorated ceiling, an unobtrusive flat white is usually the best choice. It provides good reflection and maximum flexibility. A semigloss or high gloss can be right when the ceiling is high or when you want to draw attention to decorative detail. For a high-gloss finish, the surface should be nearly perfect.

I've sometimes used pure white gloss on both walls and ceiling. This is tricky, because the effect

Partitions of stretch fabric make a private place, my bedroom.

can be too bright and sterile. But in the appropriate space, it's fresh and sparkly. It requires excellent surfaces and works better in a room that's used occasionally rather than constantly. It's good where you want a lot of light and a lively mood—in a plant room, a room off a patio (such as a breakfast room or alcove), an entertainment space (if you're the energetic type), or a room where art, photographs, crafts, or the like are on display. The harshness of the gloss can be reduced if soft colors and matte surfaces are used in the space. It will be sharpened by bright colors and reflecting surfaces.

It's usually best and always safest to paint a ceiling white. But it's fun to consider color and sometimes to use it. Color on a ceiling will cut back the light and reflect in the space, influencing its mood. A bright or strong color tends to bring down the ceiling and make the space seem smaller. A neutral, receding color (beige, taupe, blue-gray, etc.) reduces the light but doesn't affect the sense of spaciousness. It can be good in a space that's used quietly, especially in the evenings. It's also worth considering in a room that sometimes gets too much light.

A brightly colored ceiling can work well in a cheerful, informal space—a kitchen, bathroom, hall, game room. And it will distract from a poor floor or some other problem. It's tempting to try a bright color in a child's room, but children usually need all the light they've got and more. If you've got the patience, a design (such as a star map, horoscope figures, flowers, clouds) can be more practical and more attractive. Young children enjoy paint that glows in the dark.

A brightly colored border at the top of the walls will emphasize the ceiling without cutting back the light and is an interesting, quite unusual touch. However, the color and pattern will play a role in the space—if you don't know exactly how the space will develop, it's not worthwhile to limit yourself for a decorative detail. It can be added later.

Light, cool colors, such as some blues and greens, and soft colors, such as pastels, can be very pleasing on a ceiling although they, too, define the space—rather strictly. Generally I don't use them in rooms for general living or that might have art brought into them. They can be nice in a bedroom, extra parlor, dining area (if the color isn't too strong).

Dark, receding colors, such as a charcoal gray or deep blue, create intimacy, however, they're only functional in a nighttime space or one not heavily used, say, a den, foyer, dining area, bedroom. A dark ceiling between two light-reflecting ceilings will by contrast seem to recede upward.

Beamed ceilings and old wooden ceilings are popular, sometimes too much so. I've seen perfectly good plaster ceilings ripped down to expose beams that really weren't worth the effort. Then there's the problem of whether to paint the beams, which doesn't seem consistent with working so hard to expose them. Or to stain them and then paint around them, which is certainly a chore.

Old hand-hewn beams can be lovely, and should be cherished. But not every piece of wood running across a ceiling qualifies for respect. And as for fake beams stuck on for atmosphere—well, some atmosphere!

So far I've concentrated on ways of working *with* architecture, doing the best by it, not dolling it up or tearing it away. But there are times to work

The use of glass in an interior wall allows a flow of light into a darker area.

against architecture, to cover it up, disguise it, distract from it. This is usually done when something's basically wrong with the structure, or you don't have the money or time for renovation, or your home is just utterly dull.

If you have a plaster ceiling or wall that you'd like to improve, but it's too wavy and bumpy to perfect, you can apply new plaster in a swirling motion, which gives an interesting texture, rather like stucco, and camouflages the irregularities.

A fashion designer I know lived in a conventional, bland apartment that was completely out of key with his work, which is innovative and exciting. In the living room the walls have been padded with wool, which flows down over curving banquettes. The depth of the banquettes varies, so that in some places you sit almost upright, in others you lie back. The curves are arranged so that people sit turned toward each other. An organic form has been imposed upon the original rigid lines.

This is definitely not in the how-to class of home improvement. It has to be done by a pro, and it's expensive. However, you can get a somewhat similar effect with simple curved banquettes.

One of the more depressing features of modern apartments is the brown hollow-core door, with a brasslike knob with a little lock in the middle of it. Paint the door to blend in with the walls. If you can find some real doorknobs, of brass, porcelain, or the like, they're a nice touch.

In recent years, there's been a run on supergraphics—very strong geometrical arrangements of bright contrasting colors—on the walls and sometimes on the floor and ceiling as well. Supergraphics

In my loft, deep red seating platforms structure a space for large parties. They'll accommodate twenty-four people sitting in luxury. They were simple to build. Christmas lights provide enough light and the right mood.

The Joan Crawford suite at the Ambassador East Hotel—the hotel where the Pump Room is. This suite is my fantasy of the forties. A wonderful place to visit.

Facing page: The Pump Room in Chicago, which I designed while writing this book. The principles that make good clubs and restaurants popular can be applied in your own entertainment space. Note the subdued light, absence of glare, and glints of reflected light. The bar is, naturally, dark. The dining room, full of light but not harsh.

Above: Decorative light that is charming as well as illuminating. I designed these lilies.

Left: Tinted plexiglass panels in front of the windows reflect the decorative light in this space and contribute the dominant color.

Right: For sophisticated dining, one may move to a new area for coffee and dessert. For coffee or cocktails, sandblasted glass partitions mark off this more intimate space from the rest of the dining room.

In this rebuilt walkway, natural materials and sunlight create a golden hue.

Facing page: A space for collectors; the collection is integrated with the living area.

A breakfast and dining room in the interior of a New York apartment. The glass walls allow light to enter from adjacent rooms. Lights above the translucent plexiglass ceiling supplement daylight for breakfast or lunch; the chandelier is for night. The room was once a dark pantry.

can obliterate the underlying form and create new planes and angles with color alone. They're exciting. They're hard to live with.

Murals have become popular, too, and also have to be used with care. They bring depth to a space, and of course, interest. But they're very strong and can take over a space and ruin it. Stay away from the mass-produced kind. It's disappointing to find your mural in the doctor's waiting room and at the neighbor's down the street. If you're going to invest in a mural, let it be a product of your own experience and fantasies. One of my clients wanted (and got) in a playroom a scene of an old Bronx street, with candy store, grocer, etc. This was the kind of neighborhood he grew up in and loved.

There's a new process for blowing up a photograph to wall size without having it disintegrate into dots. It's still extremely expensive.

A softer way to transform a wall is to ombré it. The color can even flow across the floor and ceiling. Ombré was seen in the movie *Last Tango in Paris*: white walls with horizontal stripes running from white to cream to beige-gray to burnt orange, then back to cream and white. The trick is to have a delicate blending of color.

In rooms used at night, dark colors and/or dramatic lighting can virtually obliterate the architecture. I've even known people who were very dissatisfied with their apartments to paint them entirely black or gray or purple, and put in colored lights. This certainly creates a strong mood. But if you spend too much time in the twilight zone, you may never get back.

One of my clients lives in a Park Avenue co-op

97

An ugly ceiling transformed by a canopy.

on which the monthly maintenance costs run into five figures. You'd think the structure would be elegant, but as in so many modern apartments, structural beams and air ducts jut into the space. Her living room ceiling would be fine in a factory. The problems could be minimized by painting the walls and ceiling a quiet, neutral tone and using bright colors and shiny surfaces in the furnishings. But the ceiling can also just be covered up.

Borrowing an old idea from the French, I designed a sunburst of moiré fabric, gathered in the center with pleats radiating outward to the four corners of the ceiling. The arrangement gives the feeling of a festive tent. The height of the ceiling is lowered about a foot, but nevertheless the space is much more pleasing.

LIGHT AND LIGHTING

To really analyze and understand the space in your home, you have to be sensitive to the effect of light at different times of day and different seasons. You can't develop this sensitivity if you hide behind half-drawn drapes and gray, gritty windowpanes, and you'd be surprised how many people do. In fact, the chances are you aren't making the best use of your windows right now.

It's emotionally impossible to be satisfied with drab and dreary surroundings when sunlight is pouring in around you. When I'm working in a home, one of the first things I do is open the drapes, pull up the shades, and let in the daylight. Sometimes this reveals a depressing environment with a depressed person in it. The drawn drapes have been hiding not only worn-out upholstery and rotting lampshades, but a run-down, unhappy life. And yet once you let in the light and start cleaning and brightening, the tempo of your life will pick up as well. At least, in my experience, that's what usually happens.

With women, particularly, a dislike of light may be mixed up with a fear of getting old. There's a feeling that if one stays out of the light, no one will notice. But it just isn't so—in fact, full daylight is often more flattering than artficial light, which can emphasize lines and shadows. And musty, murky surroundings certainly don't project an image of youthful vitality.

Light creates energy, movement, and change. I recall particularly the home of a woman artist, who asked for help in making just a "few" changes. The windows were shrouded in heavy brocade drapes. When they were opened, you could see that the rest of the furnishings were also has-beens, like an old

Hollywood set. And this woman was turning into a has-been, too. Withdrawn, not working.

By the end of the year, she had a fresh, bright home. She'd lost weight. She was working again. She gave parties, had new friends. And she wasn't afraid to live with light.

Architecturally, modern windows are a sophisticated accomplishment. Not since the great stained-glass works of the late Middle Ages have there been windows as miraculous as those of our skyscrapers.

A window can be precious. It's an opening to the sky, a symbol of life and hope. No one wants to live or work in a room without windows. Ask any office manager.

So why is it that after moving into a new home people immediately buy drapes to cover up their windows? I guess drapes are even more of a status symbol than windows, especially drapes that are lined and inner-lined, trimmed with swags and jabots and fringe. I can't believe that all this still goes on. Most often it's a complete waste of energy, time, and money.

Before covering a window, think about why it's there. It has a use: to bring in light, air, and (if you're lucky) a view. It's through your windows that your home relates to the outside world.

Even a miserable window that looks out of an airshaft can let in some light. And that light is a factor in the room. Perhaps one wall is lighter than another, or a band of sunlight crosses the room for a half hour every day. A plant can live in that window.

Natural light has different qualities in different climates. For example, around the Mediterranean the light seems to be especially pervasive and to bring out the color of things as if they were lit up from inside. And light varies from the city to the country, from one side of the street to the other, from penthouse to ground floor, from morning to afternoon. Get to know the light in your home at different hours of the day and seasons of the year.

Be aware of what exposure a room has. Southern exposure will give you a bright light all day long and in all seasons. In a southern window, plants will thrive, except perhaps in the middle of summer. But you have to be careful of what fabrics you use there. In sunlight, all natural fabrics and many synthetics tend to fade and rot. Northern exposure gives the least light but an even light. The sun rises in the east, of course, so if you don't like the sun in the morning, don't put your bed near a window with an eastern exposure. But if you have a child who won't get out of bed in the morning, try it. During cocktails and dinner (in the summer), it's nice to have a view of the sunset. In the city, a view to the east, with sun shining golden in the windows, may be almost as good. In so many homes, the dining room table is in the middle of the room, with a view of nothing at all, when it could be near a window with a view to the west or east.

How much light you like to live with is a personal taste. One of my clients has all-white furnishings in her living room and dining areas, which have a full southern exposure. She enjoys more light than anyone I know. In general, southern and eastern rooms are best for the daytime, and northern and western exposures are good for evening and nighttime rooms. But it really depends on your daily sched-

ule and your personality. Some people like to sit in the dark at night near a picture window.

The purpose of curtains or anything else you put in front of a window is to control the light, and perhaps drafts, and the view in and out. The purpose is *not* to decorate the window.

If you need to cover a window, consider plain window shades, which are an elegant invention. They do exactly what they're supposed to do and nothing more. Often shades are really all a window needs. You can buy translucent ones, so that a good deal of light will come through. They also come totally opaque, and in many colors and fabrics.

Don't begin by automatically buying drapes. They may do little or nothing for you at great expense.

For example, I have a client who lives in a penthouse with a southern exposure, so she has a need to control the light, but there's no problem with people looking in, because she has no neighbors that high. When I first met her she was about to order drapery spanning twenty-five feet, and it was going to cost $3,000. It was a bad idea, not just because of the price, but because the drapes would have closed off her view; they would have made that wall very heavy; and they would have started fading within a few months and rotting within a few years. Considering what her cleaning bills were going to come to, buying these drapes would have been like investing in a car.

What she needed for the windows was something that would limit the light without closing off the view entirely, that wouldn't fade or rot, and that was easy to clean. What a bill to fill! The answer was "drapery" of bronze chains (of the key chain type,

Chain drapes allow a flow of light and air.

made with small beads). The nice thing is it doesn't do anything we didn't want it to do.

Heavy, rich drapes are not only often impractical, they're formidable; and unless you live in the Frick Museum, they're apt to seem pretentious. Also, in modern apartments air conditioners or radiators are often situated under the windows, so drapes can't be closed for most of the year. Another advantage of the chain-type drapes is that they move and shimmer in an air flow.

There are times when drapes, or more precisely floor-length curtains, are needed, usually to block a view or for insulation. (There are special inner linings designed for insulation, which will also protect the material from fading, of course.) Avoid purposeless frills or using more material than necessary. There's no point running drapes across a whole wall when all you need is to cover two windows. If you have good moldings around a window consider hanging the drapes within the frame rather than covering the moldings.

Don't use drapes in front of small windows. A friend of mine wanted to cover up a little window that looked out onto an alley, so she bought $600 worth of drapes. Naturally, everyone notices them, and walks over and opens them. A better solution would have been a translucent shade or curtain that would let in whatever light was available. Sandblasted glass or stained glass would be another possibility. A shade installed with the roller at the bottom of the window (the cord runs up and over a pulley at the top) might be good; this arrangement allows you to open the shade at the top for some light and air, without exposing the view. There are sheers, which are panels of fabric held in place by curtain rods at top and bottom. You might even try curtains made of paper clips. I've made these and they shimmer and throw interesting shadows, much like the chains.

Popular coverings for windows include venetian blinds, which can be all right, but in some rooms they seem too weighty. Today you can get lighter ones made with thin strips of brass, chrome, or other metal, or with bamboo or plastic. I was raised with the big old wooden blinds, which are heavy and clumsy but very nostalgic.

A contemporary version of venetian blinds are vertical blinds constructed of panels of metal or plastic that can be turned or folded to one side to let in light. They provide excellent light control and in the summer reflect away heat. In the evening they can be a secondary source of light, picking up reflections from the room.

Colored blinds or panels or translucent shades or curtains will cast a certain amount of color into the interior, especially in a sunny window. This can be delightful, for example, in a kitchen with a faint reddish glow in the morning.

I'm often told that drapes or curtains are needed to soften a window, but a plain window with a pleasant view is hard to improve on. However, it's true that some windows which are fine by day seem bleak at night, especially if there's little or no artificial light outside. The panes of black, opaque glass can be severe. But they can also create striking effects. A small window will reflect candles and flowers placed near it. A large window will reflect spotlighted sculpture, a chandelier, plants, and so on—often at some

Sandblasted glass can be used for windows you don't want to look out or have others looking in. It provides privacy with light.

distance. In planning a room with a picture window, check what can be reflected at night, and take advantage of the potential.

If you have land or a bit of garden outside a window, you can make a night view with outside lights. But they have to be thoughtfully placed. Very bright lights can be harmful to plants and fireflies. Too often lights are trained on a bare tree trunk or the side of a garage, when there really are more attractive vistas available. A small light on shrubbery near the window can be nicer than huge lights over acres of lawn.

Lights emphasize shapes and materials—the branches of a tree, the play of a fountain. Blue light will make your plants look healthier. Amber, red, and yellow are good directional lights, but in general they have to be used discreetly, because they tend to look like an old Grade-B technicolor movie, which is an unfortunate effect that I've seen many times.

If you have a little space around your home, but also have a problem with people looking in, first think if there's something you can do about it before covering over the window. So many windows are wasted because it's supposed to be unfriendly to put up a fence or grow a hedge. The American way of privacy is to have so much land that no one can get close enough to see in a window without trespassing. This is out of touch with reality. We have to learn how to work with and appreciate small spaces as many other cultures have been doing for centuries.

In cities, especially in poor neighborhoods, many small yards are ignored or used only as dog runs. It's depressing to see these little cemented backyards, twenty or thirty in a row, separated by chain link fences. Put them all together and there's an expanse of space that could be a pleasure for everyone.

There are two traditional window coverings that are especially attractive. Wooden shutters, particularly the kind with four shutters to the window, give excellent, flexible control of light and are also good insulation. You can open the shutters at the top for light without losing privacy, or you can fold them entirely away.

Note, when window shutters are closed, they add weight to the window wall, especially if they're unpainted wood, which is the fad these days. But originally many shutters were painted white, and there's still nothing wrong with this idea. Sometimes drapes are hung in front of shutters mainly to soften the windows. It shouldn't be necessary.

I also like lace curtains, which limit the view while letting in lots of light. And they make sexy shadows. Even though the stitching can be very elaborate, lace curtains usually have simple lines and will go with almost any style of furnishing. If you can't afford real lace, buy a synthetic. It may last longer.

Next to overfurnishing, underlighting is the most common problem in home design. By underlighting, I don't mean a lack of wattage. Often, in fact, there are places that are overlit and full of glare. But there is underuse of different light sources and a lack of flexibility and variety in lighting arrangements.

Light influences feelings and thoughts. Its effect may not be experienced consciously, but it can be very dramatic. In fact, the rhythm of our lives is controlled in part by light.

Light determines how you see the world—literally and figuratively. An ugly light (such as the fluorescent light in airports) can make you look and feel ugly. A flattering light has quite the opposite effect and can lead to romance, adventure, and other strange occurrences.

Light is at least as important to the mood and appearance of your home (and you) as material surroundings. A good light for relaxing, working, eating, talking, etc., can make an unextravagant home seem welcoming, lively, warm, and most personable.

Unfortunately, in most homes not only is the light not the best for those who live there, it's unkind to guests. Too many dining areas are lit up like a typing pool, which is bad for the digestion. Table lamps are overused and are frequently set up so there's a glare behind the person you're trying to talk with. Often, a table lamp only lights things you don't need to see, such as a full ashtray underneath it.

Sometimes to create a party mood, a host goes to the other extreme and turns off practically all the lights. Darkness doesn't automatically make for an intimate mood, or an appropriate one. Dinner, for example, shouldn't be eaten in the dark. Pitch-black restaurants seldom serve good food. For good eating and good conversation, a little light is necessary. Enjoyment of the taste of food partly depends on seeing it (in its true colors). Ideally, party light should be festive, flattering, and relaxing.

The secret to good lighting is shadows. Shadows create depth, softness, contrast, movement, and a mystique.

I know many people are frightened of changing their lighting, because it really is difficult to anticipate what the effect will be without actually installing new lights. It helps to start being aware of the light-

Traditional shutters provide flexible light control, without unnecessary weight.

ing in stores, galleries, museums, offices, etc., where the design is often more innovative than in most homes. You may find that you enjoy a brighter or dimmer light than you usually live with. Light tolerance varies widely. For example, I have very sensitive eyes and am happy with 25- or 40-watt bulbs when others want at least 60 or 75 watts.

A good lighting store or a lighting consultant may give helpful advice once you know what effect and mood you want to have. But the experts tend to advocate filling a space with an even light, which is wasteful and boring. You should have light where you need it, not elsewhere. They also tend to overuse fluorescents. The arguments in favor of fluorescents are that they're like daylight, and they last longer, and they use less electricity. But, at best, fluorescents are reminiscent of cloudy, cold daylight, and I live for sunny (and shadowy) days and moon-filled (shadowy) evenings. Florescents create no shadows. They give a cool-color, bouncing light that's the same all over. And I don't think they're kind to skin tones either. If you do need a lot of even, inexpensive light, consider the incandescent fluorescents (made by Sylvania), which are less blue and warmer than standard fluorescents.

Lighting experts also often advocate a balanced light, and this isn't always desirable. For example, if you have three lights on a track at one end of a room, you don't necessarily need three at the other end. You might, perhaps, wash the opposite wall with light.

There are two changes that would improve the lighting in 98 percent of American homes: more dimmers and fewer table lamps, at least less reliance on the standard table lamp as a major light source.

I don't think it's too much to put a dimmer on almost every single light in the home, including those in the bathrooms. The device costs less than five dollars and quickly pays for itself in electricity saved and longer life for bulbs. And a dimmer is the most basic way to achieve maximum flexibility in space use, whatever your lighting arrangements. A dimmer allows you to vary the mood from cheerful and alert to seductive and romantic. It's difficult to get this kind of change just by turning off one light after another; the result is most often too much darkness, or not enough.

Table lamps and many other standard lamps often make hot spots, that is, localized glare, which is hard on the eyes and promotes tension. And they're usually poorly placed for reading, seeing someone's face, seeing a painting, or the like. To check for hot spots, squint your eyes and look around for bright patches. A glimpse of bare bulb is always a hot spot.

Very often table lamps can be replaced to advantage by direct down light from the ceiling or from poles; indirect light, such as down light reflected off walls or wall-washing; or up light used for special effects, such as a spot shining up through a plant and throwing shadows on a wall and ceiling. However, if you do want table lamps, be sure the bulbs can't be seen. A white semiopaque or opaque lining to the shade will diffuse the light well. A shield below the bulb also does this. For working or reading, a lamp should radiate light upward as well as downward. A sharp contrast between the lit and unlit areas is tiring for the eyes. (High-intensity

108

lamps are good only as supplemental light sources in an area that is already well lit. Even so they shouldn't be used for long periods.)

If a table or standing lamp isn't on a dimmer, it helps if it has different intensities, and the lowest should be very low. Try 25 watts first.

If you dispose of one or two table lamps, you may be able to get rid of the tables as well.

Ideally, you want to have the basic light that's needed in a room on a single switch. A kitchen, of course, usually needs more basic light than a bedroom, and in general daytime rooms need more light than nighttime rooms. Then special lights are needed for special activities—over a conversation area, at a dressing table, over a chopping board, next to a reading chair. A home with numerous special lights has what's often called a "decorator's look." And it's quite possible to get too cute with these effects. I've been in kitchens where you have to turn a half dozen concealed switches in order to get enough light to cook an ordinary dinner. Most, if not all, of such working lights can be put on a single switch.

For card playing, model building or the like, an overhead pendant light is common and works quite well, but as with a reading light it should be supplemented by a more general light. There are pendant lights on a track, which provide good versatility. For example, they can be moved along the length of banquette so that you can read in any place, or along the length of a work counter in a child's room. A similar but less versatile effect can sometimes be achieved with wall lamps having flexible necks.

The best light for a dressing table or bathroom mirror is the standard theater dressing room arrange-

Down light can be subtle or dramatic.

ment, that is, incandescent bulbs (about 25 watts) set at six-inch intervals around the mirror. Again, this should be supplemented by general light—daylight, if possible.

Ideally, every storage space should be specially lit. There is a closet light attachment, in most hardware stores, that turns off the closet light when the door is closed, turns it on when the door opens.

If you have art or hobbies on display, each item should be adequately lit. Good lighting does more for a painting than a fancy frame. Dark shelves are no place for small artifacts. Shelves can be backlit through white acrylic or lit by lights from the ceiling, such as swivel lights.

Plants can be lit by down light, or up light from the base of the planter or, if they're in a niche, from the side.

The greatest difference between professional and amateur lighting is that professionals use light for dramatic and decorative effect, whereas the amateur is satisfied if there's enough light to see what he's doing. If you light something as if it were important and spectacular, it will seem that way. An ordinary conversation area becomes exciting when lit with two opposite beams of light shining down at a 45-degree angle. (Note, this is evening lighting. In the day, you'll need more light in the space, or you'll find your guests gazing out the windows as if they were wishing they were out there.)

The most orderly, unobtrusive, and luxurious type of down light is recessed ceiling light. If this is possible in your home, and right for the architecture, you should consider it. The job should be done by an electrical contractor.

For most homes, track lights are a far more prac-

Down light can be subtle or dramatic.

Recessed down light and a small banquette transform an awkward corner.

112

tical form of down light. Their design has been improved lately, so that the fixtures aren't so bulky and industrial-looking. Now they come in many colors, so you probably won't have to do what I've done in the past—paint the fixtures to blend with the ceiling.

The advantages of track lights are: (1) They're not expensive. (2) They're flexible. The tracks can go on wall or ceiling; the lights rotate; many of the fixtures are interchangeable; you can get a variety of light, from pinpoint beams to fairly diffuse light. (3) If you're fairly handy, you can probably do without professional installation. The lights can be on a single switch or on individual switches.

Track lights can be used for either direct or indirect light (when the light is bounced off a wall). The indirect light they provide is usually considerably brighter than people imagine—if you haven't used this kind of light before, begin with about half the number of fixtures you think you'll need. It may be enough. The direct light can be the means of lighting cabinets, closets, and other murky spots. Some kinds of track lights come with colored lenses and different grids for making patterns (weaves, polka dots, etc.). Track lights should never cause hot spots; they're available with recessed lenses that diffuse the light.

A variety of light sources is intriguing. Every home needs decorative light, which is like seasoning in cooking. Candles on a dining room table, reflections in a mirror or a metal surface, the light of an aquarium—all are sources of decorative light that enhance the appeal of a room. (Candles shouldn't be saved for guests only—they're a small investment for pleasanter meals.)

Wall-washing provides basic, indirect light, but it is primarily a decorative technique, and a very striking one. A lighted wall will be a dominant element in a space, and therefore it will draw attention away from awkward architectural features, such as too many door and window openings. However, it should then be balanced by some other lighting source, such as a bold overhead fixture in another part of the room.

Watch out for lighting a wall that's behind or close to seating. It's uncomfortable to relate to silhouettes. Except in a hallway, a washed wall should have some space in front of it.

I love Christmas lights, and I use them for their decorative appeal. Maybe I enjoy them so much because my house is in downtown Manhattan, where it's almost as dark at night as in the country, and I want some lights to remind me of Fifth Avenue and Broadway.

I use strands of small white Christmas lights at the top of a wall or along the baseboard. Sometimes I recess them behind a picture molding, but more often not. They provide less practical light than wall-washers, but they're quite good enough to light a hall, and more informal. In my own home I also have strung them along the ceiling beams in our living space.

Incidentally, I've always been told there's a problem with Christmas lights burning out, but I've never encountered one. I use the constant lights, not the ones that twinkle (too jumpy), and I keep some strands burning twenty-four hours a day. The bulbs last literally for years—I have some that have lasted for more than four years.

With the use of color spots or wall-washers, you transform the tone and mood of a space. However,

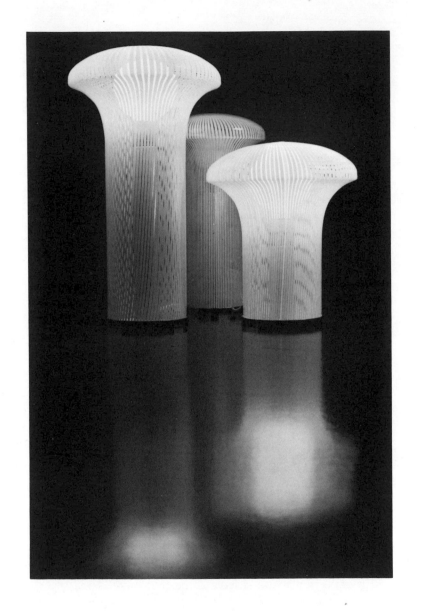

114

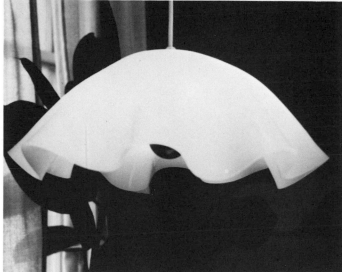

Ideally, a light should be beautiful in itself.

don't flood a room with color because sitting in a pool of color, with everyone looking green or blue, isn't pleasing. You can get a good feeling of color by lighting one wall, crossing spotlights on the ceiling, or the like. (If you have quite a lot of color in the room to begin with, check the color mix before committing yourself. The effect may look like mud.)

Colored lights enhance certain fabrics. For example, I have a client who has placed a white satin chaise near a wall washed with blue light. When she turns on the washers, the satin seems to glow.

Neon lights are available in many types, from custom installations to existing (old) signs. The problem with neon in the past has been that the intensity is very strong. But at last a dimmer device has been made for it.

I have to mention now that central overhead fixtures, which should be *pièces de résistance* in lighting, are most often a disaster. The old chandelier designs have not adapted well to electricity. They were made to glitter with candles, and flame-shaped bulbs are no substitute. Contemporary designs tend to be ugly and expensive. There are exceptions, of course. For example, I've liked and used lights from Italy designed by Venini. They have a series of handsome lights made with transparent rose or gray glass and chrome with opaline bulbs. But most often I design my own for a specific space, often using ordinary objects such as inverted fishbowls (with showcase bulbs inside). I think almost any person who tries can do as well with his own design as at most stores.

Years can go by without any change in the lighting of a home. People repaint, reupholster, etc., but keep the light the same. "A new light" means a fresh start. Show yourself in a new light more often.

COLOR

Decorators get a lot of business from people who're worried about colors and patterns. To read some of the advice columns on the subject, you'd think the main problem in arranging a home is deciding what goes best with avocado or whether you can put stripes near polka dots.

I love color, but it can be a very heavy statement. A little bit goes a long, long way.

You can see the impact of small amounts of color in some fabric weaves. In good tweeds, for example, the color of a single accent thread can determine the final impression. A black line against beige and brown creates a serious mood. Change the thread to red and the effect is totally different.

Color together with light (another form of color) sets the mood of space. Color seems to touch the emotions directly. Certain shades of green, purple, and brown are often experienced as depressing, whereas yellow, orange, and red tend to be stimulating.

A very common mistake, once you decide what mood and color you want in a space, is then to lay on too much. The color becomes oppressive. You're stuck with it. You can't turn it off.

In a new home the empty rooms can seem so austere that you want to give them warmth. And color creates instant intimacy. But a room will have quite a different feeling when it's lived in and filled with things and people. As a friend of mine said, "Color is generally a background for something else —unless you want a wall as a friend."

Just as I started to write this section, a young woman I know made the classic mistake with color. She moved into an attractive, newly renovated apartment after breaking up with the man she'd been living with. Naturally, she wanted this apartment to give a message to the world ("I'm feminine, single, and self-sufficient, and not necessarily unfriendly, if you're nice"). Her apartment is probably listed as three and a half rooms, but it's what I'd call a large two rooms. She picked a strong pink for the bedroom and a comparably strong peach for the living/dining/kitchen room. Emotionally, the colors were an important statement at the time she chose them. They were also interesting. On a color chart, the effect was good. On the walls it was awful. She moved in at the beginning of December. On January 1, hung over, she started painting the walls white. There was too much color and no place to get away from it. Moreover, the colors were demanding. Every single thing in the space ought to have been keyed to them, but she wasn't about to go out and buy all new furniture and fabrics.

I know lots of people who'd never make a mistake like that. With them it's all white, white, white, (or beige, beige, beige) and safe, safe, safe. White and beige *are* safer, and I work with both of them a great deal myself. Light neutral shades in the background allow the introduction of any color and mood. And in the evening, when daylight fades, the space doesn't suddenly become somber and gloomy.

But white is also bleak and beige is bland. When they're overused I'm reminded of Bill Blass's remark that bad taste is better than no taste at all. The eye and the soul need color. But how much? And where?

After painting a few walls white, my friend with the new apartment then decided it was starting to look too plain, and went out to shop for wallpaper. I've been trying to convince her that if she makes a mistake now, it's going to be much harder to correct. Wallpaper is many times more difficult to work with than simple paint, especially when you only have a couple of rooms. It usually introduces not just one color but two or three. *And* a pattern. And often a theme, such as little ladies ice-skating, or twining roses, or a Japanese landscape. Some wallpaper patterns are just ruinous.

To an important degree, how much color to bring into your home depends on how much space you have, how it's divided, and how it's used. As a rule, the more space you have, the more freedom you have with color. If you're a restrained person, not the type to make a splash, the danger is depriving yourself of color, living against a dull or even muddy background. If you love color and aren't afraid of it, the danger is excessive exuberance. It can be catastrophic to try to force moods through color alone. The surfaces in your home aren't potential color photographs or canvases to be covered. *You* are going to be part of that space. And you should be important in it. And comfortable. Not overwhelmed. A brilliant showcase is nice to look at in a department store. It's less nice when you're living within it.

The first step in deciding on colors for a home is to become sensitive to the many beautiful and unusual colors in the world—there is literally an infinite number. Then you should select a collection of colors you love without worrying about how you'll work them into your home. Don't assume that your old favorite colors are still your favorites. People's tastes in color change, and now you may enjoy colors you didn't care for previously. Colors for a home are usually chosen from much too narrow a spectrum, without exposure to the range of possibilities. No color should be eliminated from consideration on principle. Any color you love you can have in your home.

It's essential to understand what spectrum and intensity of colors you enjoy most. One approach is to look at the clothes you own. The chances are they'll include your favorite colors. Prints are usually chosen primarily for the combination of colors and only secondarily for the patterns. They often give a good indication of a person's color taste. (Men who wear conservative clothes will learn more from their ties and sport shirts than their suits.)

In helping a client choose colors, I frequently work with Color-Aid cards, which are available at art stores. These are five by eight colored cards, and I present them at random. You can get a set for yourself, relax with a drink or whatever, and start picking the colors that appeal to you. Give yourself a couple of hours to make your choices. Too many important decisions about a home—that have to be lived with for years—are made under time pressure.

Most people end up with a selection of ten to twenty-five colors, and these can usually be arranged to flow into one another. It's quite rare for a person to choose incompatible colors. This means that theoretically you could use all the colors you like. But unless you live in a chateau, you'll have to narrow down to a few, perhaps two or three in a single-space home, a half dozen in an average family house. You may then bring in other colors, but these will be the key ones.

Another good way to select colors is from fabrics—fabrics of all sorts, not just upholstery—for these come in a far greater variety of hues than the standard paints, wallpapers, or other materials specifically designed for the home. When you find a

119

color you like, buy a good-sized piece of the fabric so you can judge the impact of the color in the space.

It's practically impossible to make imaginative, good decisions on the basis of tiny swatches of material or those little squares of paint they show you in paint stores. No one can figure out from a one- or three-inch sample what an entire wall or room will look like. Find colors you like and have the paint mixed to match them. A very fine painter will mix paint for you and paint a couple of feet of wall so you can see what it will look like when dry. If you're buying your paint and bringing it home, buy the smallest amount possible and paint a sample of the wall yourself to be sure. And use a store that will adjust the color for you.

I'm not trying to create make-work when I say study colors before making plans. Paint stores and fabric dealers generally have a few shades they're pushing each season. And these shades run to fads. If you set out with only a vague idea that you'd like a light blue or an off-white, you're going to be rushed into a decision on the spot, and you'll be making your selection from a very limited number of choices. For example, in the fifties turquoise and chartreuse were in for a while, then olive green. In the sixties there was a run on the primary and secondary colors, in pure, intense, hard-rock shades. In the seventies there's been more interest in soft, unusual mixed colors.

At home there's no reason to have colors you can see everywhere else. You should have your own unique color environment, colors you take pleasure in.

Of course, most people don't deliberately decide to live with the same color scheme as everyone else, so why is there so little variety? The answer is com-

plex, because reactions to color are determined by many factors, including culture and social class, to say nothing of the desire to be fashionable.

For example, I've mentioned that in eighteenth-century France the dominant colors were delicate pastels, white, and gold, which expressed the cultural importance of luxury and leisure and the disdain for practical considerations, such as coffee stains. In our century, the neutral, colorless environments associated with the Bauhaus and (often) Scandinavian modern reflect our concern with function and materials and our de-emphasis of frivolity and fantasy. Other factors may also be significant. For example, psychologist Charles Winick has said that the popularity of beige is related to the melding of sexual roles, the fading of sexual distinctions.

At any rate, for a variety of reasons, light tan and white are high-status colors. And, like the French aristocracy's pastels, their use is a form of conspicuous consumption, since they're difficult to maintain, especially in the cities. In Chicago or New York a white rug or a white linen suit in summer is overtly extravagant. Also, pale, neutral shades are obviously worlds away from the bright colors favored by lower-status, lower-class groups.

Lately, there has been some reaction against bland, monotonous, neutral interiors. I recently heard a Puerto Rican executive on television say that coming back to New York from the island always sent him into shock from color starvation. I knew what he meant. It was winter and cold and gray, and midtown was all concrete and glass outside and beige carpet and chrome inside. We do need more color. But we don't need those standardized, unpleasant greens, pinks, and blues used in so many furnished rooms and modest homes. They represent an attempt to literally brighten dreary lives, to bring interest into a space where there's nothing else interesting.

In a more sophisticated way decorators often fall into the same trap: using loads of color to artificially create something interesting in a space that's intrinsically uninteresting. Once in a while, this might even be defensible as a stopgap measure. But it's seldom a satisfactory long-term solution. It's preferable to plan for a small amount of very beautiful color. The color will be clearer and more dramatic if it doesn't have to compete with the entire rainbow.

There's also the role of gender in color preferences. Men feel comfortable with "masculine" colors: gray, black, white, brown, dark green, maroon, dark blue. Many women favor the "feminine" colors: the pastels and bright colors (red, yellow, orange, purple). But women tend to be more versatile and can move into the masculine spectrum as well.

There are entire countries that seem to be masculine or feminine in their color tastes; for example, England and Germany most often use masculine colors, Switzerland and France use more feminine colors.

And colors are associated with certain personality types and styles of behavior, so much so that it may be almost physically impossible for you to live with colors you connect with an image you dislike.

For instance, a bright red is challenging, daring, and exhibitionistic. However, it's less bold inside the home than outside. Even when no man would ever have worn red to the office, red slippers and a red smoking jacket were traditional. But then and now many men prefer their reds muted to maroon, rust, or the like.

Similarly, many women feel uncomfortable wearing a bright red or having much of it in the home. Red is the traditional color of the sexually aggressive woman, the fallen woman, of Carmen and Hester Prynne. But as you lighten red to pink, the associations are increasingly with feminine sweetness rather than boldness.

Black is also a strong color and has erotic overtones, and black with red is a powerful combination that has to be used discreetly. Moreover, the sweetness of pink or, say, lavender is utterly lost when combined with black. The combination is very popular for sexy underwear; I suppose because it suggests the "good" woman is also "bad."

Navy blue is the ultimate conservative color. Black and white together are also conservative and make an impression of self-assurance, energy, sophistication, and lack of warmth. Earth colors (browns, dark greens, terra cottas, etc.) are informal but slightly stuffy. Mixed middle shades, such as olive green, gold, and some of the blue greens belong in the living rooms of successful businessmen who're always tired after dinner.

Many of your own personal associations with and reactions to color may be too strong to change. But if you examine them, you'll probably find that some old prejudices can be thrown out.

Start *seeing* colors again, instead of just half-consciously registering their existence. Look around you. Look for colors you've never seen before. Look for colors you love and start collecting samples of them. As you become more sensitive to color, you may actually want less of it around you. The colors that you do care for, you'll want to present strikingly.

If you feel insecure about your color sense, don't

force it. Do only one wall at a time. Or cover only one piece of furniture at a time. Gradually you'll learn which colors you live with best and how to balance them. There's no substitute for this experience, but here are some of the ideas I keep in mind when helping clients choose colors.

First, if you have a general feeling that you like a particular color, say, red, then look at reds in all tints and shades. Tinting a color is adding white (so the tints of red run from red to pink to white). Shading a color is adding gray or black. Also study the color's different hues. How much yellow can be added to red and still give you a good red feeling? How much blue? I find that often a mixed, soft color is more appealing to a client than the pure color—and, of course, a lot more can be used. Some of the very lightest shades can be used almost as freely as neutral colors, for example, a very pale, soft lemon yellow, or blue gray or gray green. They remain discreetly in the background and don't interfere with most art, patterned fabrics, or whatever you might later put into the space. But even these lighter shades do influence a mood.

Incidentally, very light colors with white trim and a white ceiling don't cut down significantly on light, certainly no more than a receding neutral shade, such as dark cream or taupe.

The impact of a color will depend on its brightness, or intensity, and the other colors near it. All colors look stronger in contrast to white or black. If you want to mute the impact of a color, you need a soft gray or beige near it, not black or white.

Juxtaposing complementary or primary colors also makes a bold effect. In some cases the effect may be loud (as with the complementary yellow and pur-

ple), but it's harmonious. The American flag is a good example of how to obtain maximum boldness; use two pure primary colors accented with white.

The hot colors (those with yellow or red) are stimulating and energizing, sometimes too much so. These are high-value colors that attract the eye and reflect strongly into the surrounding space. They don't recede, they jump out. They make other colors recede by comparison. Both, but particularly red, have to be used with caution.

Cool colors have blue in them and, except for the very bright shades, tend to have a quieting, relaxing effect. Green is less cold than blue and also is generally a calming color.

With pastels, most people worry that they may be too soft, insipid, wishy-washy. But in fact they can be quite strong. Generally, when I'm using pastels in any quantity—on a wall, for example—I stay with the pale shades. Then for clarity and crispness, I might contrast the pastel with white woodwork and a white ceiling or a white or natural rug.

A traditional and still pleasing way of painting a room is to use a dark color on the walls with white trim and a white ceiling. This combination emphasizes the architectural character of a space and is most appropriate in a well-proportioned, well-detailed room. In the past, apparently, people could tolerate sitting in dark rooms in daytime. But I use dark colors only in nighttime rooms, for the color imposes a pervasive indoor mood.

Dark colors are popular, because they're quiet, wear well, are easy to maintain. So some warnings are in order. If you're shopping for dark paint, it's essential to be cautious about the standard mixes. Many are unpleasant. The blues, for example, are often too electric or too black. But there are hundreds of possible shades to choose from, if you take the care to search them out.

Each decade recently has had a chic dark color: dusty rose in the forties, hunter green in the fifties, chocolate brown in the sixties; in the seventies, eggplant, or "aubergine" if you want to be fancy. It's a big step to paint a wall a dark color, so having a popular one is reassuring. But as I've said, if you can see it everywhere else, you don't need it at home.

Dark or medium-value colors can quickly be overused. For example, if you fill a space with medium-value greens, browns, and reddish browns, the feeling can be down, depressing. Such colors kill light. You'll need a bright color or white or very light shades to pick up the mood.

Dark colors recede. A charcoal gray ceiling in most lights is hard to define—it's hard to see exactly where the ceiling begins. For this reason it's often assumed that dark colors are unobtrusive. But it doesn't always work that way. Darkness also is heavy; it adds weight to a space. A dark piece of furniture—for example, a navy blue sofa—can be like a black hole in the middle of your living room. This is especially true if the sofa is in front of a light-colored wall or on a light rug.

The most common mistake in the use of dark colors is putting dark drapes on windows. I've just finished removing a set of green velvet drapes from a client's living room. The material was lovely. But windows are sources of light and should contribute a feeling of openness. With these weighty dark drapes in front of it, the window wall became gloomy, the whole room was darker.

In using dark and light colors together, you have to consider how much contrast you want. Contrasts are exciting, not relaxing. They'll interfere with soft or delicate effects. To a certain extent you can puncture the impact of contrast with touches of other color. For example, if a navy sofa is against a white wall, beige cushions will make the effect less stark.

I create contrast for the person who is comfortable with it, which is usually someone who's dynamic, strong, and definite. For example, I made a high-contrast seating area (black marble table, burnt orange banquette, natural cotton on the walls) for a young businessman who's made a large success with his own company. He's at home in this space. I'd considered a monochromatic décor, but it seemed too cautious for his personality.

Contrast is dramatic. It draws attention. It can be used to underline the best features in a space, or to focus on a particular area. For example, in the pictures of one of the homes in the color section you see in the middle of the living room a dark green and dark purple ottoman. There's almost no other color. This draws the eye to the middle of the room. The area is center stage.

But contrast is fixed and unyielding. It requires good, exact shapes. A strong contrast area is a sure way of making an impression. But it can also create too much tension to be comfortable.

Another tempting way to impress with color is by matching. It's especially tempting if you're insecure about colors, because with matching you don't have to worry about mixing. But it can be hard to get an exact match, and a near miss can be disconcerting. And when you do get a perfect match, who notices?

A flower garden isn't created with matching colors. A red rose isn't the same red throughout. Matching is an artificial effect. It has a place but not a great one. More beauty is found in the flow and nuance of colors.

Have confidence in your ability to find a variety of colors that harmonize. Most people do not on their own choose colors that are dissonant. They go wrong only when they start pushing for a color effect they've seen in a magazine or department store.

The trickiest color combinations involve either the same color at different intensities (for example, maroon, scarlet, and pink) or the same base color mixed with two different colors (for example, certain blue greens against certain yellow greens). Such combinations shouldn't be ruled out. They're worth looking at. They can be extraordinarily striking. But work with samples in your space (and in the different lights that they'll be seen in). Don't feel you should be able to figure it out in your head or over the counter.

Generally, it's difficult to combine pastels with purer colors, and such combinations are seldom attempted. It can be done with contrasting colors when one is used as an accent (for example, a bright red against a very pale green background). It is also possible to create a flow from a pastel to a purer color when working with a large space or moving from room to room. For example, in the summer house I worked on in Nantucket, the foyer is creamy white; then there are two parlors, one apricot and white, the other pumpkin and white; in the kitchen, the ceiling, the table, the insides of the cabinets are a watermelon red, and other important surfaces are stainless steel. Note, though, that the colors were used with restraint and balanced with a lot of white.

After choosing your colors you have to relate them to your home. The ideal is a variety of colors and moods; of light, bright, and dark; cheerful, energetic, and quiet. In planning color, I believe it's helpful to think in terms of these moods, of what you want of lightness and darkness, intensity and quiet, rather than worrying about particular colors. If you have a balance and flow of mood, the colors usually take care of themselves.

In a single space, however, only so much color can be accommodated without confusion. A single-space home, such as a studio apartment, is probably the most difficult for color planning, especially when there isn't as much light as you'd like. It can be catastrophic to impose a definite mood with color, even if the mood is cheerfulness, sweetness, or vigor.

I usually recommend light, neutral colors for a studio apartment, at least for the background surfaces. Tranquility is essential. And a small space has to be flexible and coherent.

And yet, as a rule, color variety is needed. Leaving the space entirely neutral may bring on color starvation. Introducing just one color is an approach which can be dramatic, but it's very severe. Leaving the walls neutral and the ceiling white, I would usually try to work in two or three dark colors (such as a dark purple, a darkish green, a navy blue) and a couple of lighter and/or brighter colors (such as lemon yellow, apricot, lime green).

Additional color can be introduced with colored lights, which allow you to have a party mood you can turn off in the morning. A blue light can be shone up through a tall green plant, or a wall washed with yellow or orange light.

Lofts, although often essentially single-space homes, can take more color because of their size. However, in a dark loft—and many are very dark—a bright white is welcome and is often the best base color. In loft spaces you can use colored fabric in creating partitions, either stretched from floor to ceiling or fabric wrapped around plywood panels. Colored acrylic panels can be hung from hooks, or you can simply paint plywood. Colored lights (for example, blue, soft lavender, or pale green) can be used to set off a quiet, private place. A discotheque feeling for entertaining can be evoked with a dance platform lit by contrasting pure colors (red, yellow, blue).

Thus color can function to differentiate areas in a large space. In my home, five floating maroon banquettes create the seating space for parties. The color defines the space and draws in people. It looks warm (and feels the same, because the upholstery is piled velvet).

In a two- or three-room apartment it's still important to keep the public space tranquil and open to different moods, but in a bedroom or workroom a more personal mood and more color is appropriate if wanted. Color on the floor can be good, or, if you like a subdued room, a dark-colored ceiling. And you can use intense and moody colors that might be too strong in a public space.

In larger homes, five or six rooms or more, you have that much more freedom in the amount of color you can use. But aesthetically the aim is still to maintain a pleasant flow of color. This sometimes means, when a family is involved, that a conflict comes up between the designer's standards of style and the preferences of different individuals. I'd have to say that the needs of individuals are more important. A child may want colors and a mood inimical to the rest of the décor. And so may anyone in a private space. In a large home, there's no reason not to give life to fantasies, to have a Hollywood dressing room or a Rolling Stones den.

If a child chooses a problematic color, I usually show him other possibilities, such as lighter or darker versions of that color, not to force him to change, but to educate him. Most children are very open and free about color once they get involved. And if the room is really out of key with the rest of the home, the transition can be eased by a neutral color in the adjacent space, or perhaps a shaded version of the difficult color.

Even in a large home I like to have several light, neutral spaces, usually the entertainment or gathering places. And even in a highly colored space, I often like to have natural shades to accentuate the color, for instance, a natural rug and white blinds when the walls are a medium or dark color.

Strong, bright hues are focal points of energy. They wake you up. In a single-space home a couple of touches of sharp color pick up the mood. In a multi-space home, it's good to have a few different strong-color areas.

Bright colors can work very well in halls (which are so often sad and neglected). They're exciting, they make you pay attention to your surroundings, they set up a mood of anticipation, of coming into a special place with special people. I did one hall recently with a bright red ceiling (which helped to distract from the dark entrance and quite poor, uneven walls).

125

I did another with yellow walls, a purple ceiling, and white gloss woodwork. It gives a terrific jolt. Walking through the hall is an event instead of a transition. (However, a hall does have to relate to the adjacent space. It would be distressing to walk out of a strong, youthful, primary-color hall into a sedate green and gold parlor.)

There's some logic to the choice of bright, hot colors for kitchens and bathrooms. But they shouldn't be used with abandon. They reflect on the food and the skin. The traditional yellow is good, although often applied in too dark a shade. For a feeling of clarity and cleanliness in a kitchen, an excellent choice is white, sometimes a high-gloss white. This is pleasant for working but too bright for relaxed eating.

Another appropriate place for bright colors can be a game room, especially in a dark basement. Also any area where physical work is done—a laundry room, garage, or the like.

Medium-value colors and pastels may be good in semiprivate or private spaces: bedroom, study, den, or parlor. If you have a large, formal, relatively achromatic entertainment space, then a more intimate, warmer space is nice for small gatherings. Most people enjoy moving from a small, relatively highly colored space into a more expansive, undefined environment, and vice versa. It's like the indoors versus the outdoors. No one wants to be just indoors or just outdoors all the time; it's pleasant to move back and forth.

I also sometimes use medium-value or even bright colors in dining areas, a burnt orange, for example, or a forest green. I might do one wall or the chairs or the table—but I'd try to avoid a heavy atmosphere of color. Most often, I use very little color,

if any. Candles, flowers, glassware, silver can by themselves bring a lovely, bright feeling into the space. There's no need to rely on color to set the mood.

Dark moods, as I've said, I prefer in nighttime rooms. I've done a den with plum walls, orange and wheat upholstery, and a white rug. Similarly, a man's library with gray walls and ceiling, a red and green stripe around the ceiling, and an Oriental rug. Both these homes had light and airy living rooms and needed a secluded quiet room for relaxing. For people who like darkness, I've gone so far as to build rolling panels to cover the windows. In one such case, I then painted the walls with a white lacquer gloss, so there was a feeling of freshness even though there was none (except via the air conditioner).

Babies' rooms can be bright, with quite a lot of pure primary and secondary colors, which infants love. Older children also tend to choose bright, obvious colors, but often they aren't comfortable with them for long. I do believe in letting the child make the decision, but sometimes I can see trouble ahead. For example, I worked with one boy who wanted red, white, and blue: red walls, blue ceiling, white curtains. His room was nine by twelve and he needed to do his homework there as well as sleep and play. At his mother's insistence, he got the room he wanted. And within two weeks he was doing his homework in the den on a card table, and his toys were beginning to spread throughout the house. He was spending less and less time in his room. I sat down with him, and then we repainted the room with white walls, red ceiling, blue molding—and he moved back again.

Although I believe in conservative color rules, quite often I find reasons to break my own rules.

I designed an office retreat for a woman entirely in pink, quite a strong pink. I don't think many people could stand this, but she thrived on it. It helped her work. It made her feel good. (Incidentally, this office was written up in the *New York Times* in an article on my client. It's much easier for a designer to get publicity for his flashy work than for his quiet work, which may be one reason why so much flashy work is done.)

I painted a bedroom of my own entirely a medium blue. I was living in the old Lit Brothers house in Philadelphia. The room was very large, with a glass dome in the ceiling. Needless to say, for the first week I was wide-eyed every morning at five. I like my bedroom to be enveloping, relaxing, sensual —*not* bright and lively. The solution was blue walls, green palms, and hanging planters (to cut some of the light and produce shadows).

Blue is a good bedroom color for many people. A sky blue is relaxing in a low light and cheerful in daylight. It can work well on the ceiling.

In a suburban house on Long Island I designed a bedroom/lounge suite in a converted attic, with a white gloss on walls and ceiling. If one of my students suggested gloss in a bedroom, I'd probably flunk him. But this space had very unusual, striking angles, and we had rebuilt it on three different levels and added five skylights. (It consists now of a sleeping area, library area, and walk-in storage.) With the skylights and the white gloss, the original hot, dark attic now looks and feels bright, light, and fresh. The brilliant white, which is lit from different levels, draws attention to the unique architecture. Numerous plants and one spot of bright color (a sherbety apricot in the lounge) prevent the space from seeming stark.

I generally don't like to try to patch over problems with cheery colors, but sometimes I do anyway. Color brightens and distracts and can be used in a playful way to enliven dull architecture. In homes where there are no moldings, I sometimes paint a stripe around the top of the walls (and even run it down the wall and across upholstery). In a space with awkward proportions or odd angles, a colored wall can provide a focal point that integrates the shape. In a narrow space the tunnel effect can be alleviated by painting the end wall a bright color, or by running one or more stripes of color vertically on the end wall or across the floor. In a room with a high ceiling, you can bring down the ceiling visually by painting it a medium shade; if the color's the same as that of a rug, there's a warm reflection and an attractive contrast in texture. In a kitchen that had built-in ochre yellow porcelain appliances and dusty yellow floor tiles and lemony yellow plastic laminate counters and dark wood cabinets (!), I painted the walls white and the ceiling a bright lime. This helped to override the mix and match that didn't match.

For a woman who lived in a small, dark studio apartment and wanted a complete and dramatic change, I used color everywhere, even on the ceiling. Not brilliant color, which she couldn't have lived with, but soft pastels. The ceiling is a soft lavender, the walls a soft tangerine, the carpeting a sharp celery green and the lounge seating is slipcovered in light lemon yellow and white. It worked. She felt wonderful about it. And it won't be expensive to change when she wants something new.

Freedom in combining colors is very much reduced when the element of pattern is added. We have survived, fortunately, the greatly publicized "pattern on pattern" look. It made good copy but rarely good living.

The difficulty of working with patterns is exploited by designers and retailers who offer miles of matching fabrics or preselected mix-and-match patterns that are supposed to look casual and spontaneous, but more often look synthetic and cute.

I generally recommend staying away from patterns in the basic planning for any multiuse space, and being very careful of them altogether. There are subtle patterns inherent in different textures. And as a space is lived in, patterns will emerge in ways that aren't easy to visualize—in the arrangement of art, cushions, knickknacks, bookcases, and so on. To be successful most highly patterned spaces have to be kept almost empty of the paraphernalia of living.

Women have to be particularly careful in using patterns, since the hard sell on patterns is always aimed at them. Too often a woman shopper comes home with a roomful of patterned paper and fabric that most men can't stand.

When I give such severe advice, I'm often told that the client longs for floral designs, gay ginghams and so on. I agree 100 percent that flowers are lovely, and if you must have a floral pattern, then buy a beautiful piece of fabric and enjoy it. But first consider another way to bring flowers into a home—flowering plants, cut flowers, dried flowers. I also enjoy fine silk flowers, which I think of as art, not imitation.

My warnings about patterns aren't because I dislike them—actually I enjoy them—but because they're hard to live with over time. At the moment I'm redesigning the suites in the Ambassador East Hotel in

Quality of color counts more than quantity. These banquettes set different tones. The red is strong, rich, and suggests a night mood. The pale apricot is delicate and suited for daylight; in a dark space or near strong colors it would be lost.

*For dining, not too much color,
a festive light, a round table.*

*Facing page: If two colors in a
space are enough, don't add
more.*

A dream living room—all the glitter of the city without confusion or noise. Lights and mirrors are the key elements: the ceiling is mirrored; the coffee table consists of two mirrors treated so that they reflect an infinity of lights; the subtle tones and patterns of the rug are soft.

Facing page: A private lounge for two. The original architecture of the room is submerged in organic forms. The room is utterly quiet, completely soundproofed. (The cat is an Oriental headrest, an invitation to stretch out.)

For this boudoir, what other color but pink? But even here, a quiet pink.

A study with a warm light and a masculine style. The copper shades and lamp base and the bronze-tinted mirror are important secondary light sources at night.

Chicago. It's a famous old hotel known for attracting famous visitors like Joan Crawford and Queen Elizabeth, Frank Sinatra and Zsa Zsa Gabor. I'm using lots of patterned fabric on the walls, slipcovers, and draperies. We're recreating the thirties and forties, when the hotel was the very last word, and there's no reason not to have fun and try out some extreme effects. Visitors don't have to live with these patterns. For a few nights they can enjoy a mystique which has otherwise passed from the scene.

If you're not starting from scratch with a home but are trying to improve a place that's already furnished, then there are limits on what you can do about the color. In fact, a decorator might advise you that nothing can be done unless you throw out all your furniture and repaper your walls. Not so.

First decide whether the areas in your home have approximately the right tone. Is the kitchen light and bright enough? Would you like the bedroom more subdued? Is the dining area intimate and relaxing? Is the living room cheerful or bland and boring? Is there any space you can't stand to be in, and, if so, is color the main problem? Is there a space you especially love, and, if so, is it because there's beautiful color in it?

Give first attention to the space you care about most. (I'd say this should be the space you spend most time in, but I know everyone worries first about the space guests use.) Consider next the space you like least. Not only is it a relief to do something to a miserable area, but often the most creative changes take place here, precisely because there isn't much one wants to keep the same.

Silk flowers rather than flowery fabrics.

Don't forget halls, basement, or other areas used only in passing or occasionally. They can take a lot of color, even patterns.

As for your furniture, forget about (and, if possible, throw out) the pieces you don't really care for. Concentrate on the ones you want to keep forever. The color of these pieces you love must be right in the space. Either the walls, floor, and ceiling harmonize with this furniture or something drastic has to be done. If you have an eight-foot sofa that's perfect except for the color, begin by getting it recovered before thinking of redoing the walls. Otherwise, when you finally find the ideal fabric for the sofa, it may not go with the newly painted walls.

Consider moving around some of the furnishings. Typically, all the best pieces in a home are crowded into the living room, which is overfurnished, while the rest of the home has to make do with the leftovers. Many living rooms are ruined by an Oriental rug in say, striking blue, red, gold, and cream. Nothing else goes with it. But why does it have to be in the living room? Would it work in a bedroom? Or on a hall wall?

In working with a home that's already furnished, don't be too casual. Practice the same restraint and discretion you would use if designing from the beginning. Above all, simplify. The aim isn't to get the maximum possible number of colors into a space. Rather, present a few lovely colors, individually— that's real style.

FURNITURE AND FURNISHINGS

After you've analyzed your space, its architecture and character, then you can realistically begin to plan your furnishings. Remember, you are not buying furniture to fill up space; you aren't buying it to please your neighbors; and, unless you really know what you're doing, you probably aren't buying it as an investment. Furniture is to be lived with, used, and eventually worn out, at least in most cases.

I say this without much hope of reforming anyone's buying habits. Having been directly and indirectly involved in the furniture business for years, I've seen overpriced, nonfunctional furniture sell and sell and sell. Few customers ever question the necessity or desirability of buying certain pieces, of achieving a certain look. On television, in magazines, in display rooms in department stores, you've seen thousands, probably tens of thousands, of different "homes." But there's incredibly little variety. Even modest homes have wall-to-wall carpets, drapes, a large sofa, big bureaus in the bedrooms, a dining room set, and so on.

One way to cleanse the mind of preconceived ideas of what should be in your home is to imagine you are creating all the furnishings yourself. What do you need? Something to sit on and sleep on, surfaces for eating and working, storage units, perhaps curtains for privacy, and a rug if the floor is cold. You need color and something beautiful to look at. You probably want to have around some items of personal and sentimental value. But if you were designing from scratch, would you bother with finial knobs on étagère shelves or a valance over the drapes? What would they contribute?

Furniture and the styles of furnishings reflect the society in which they're made. Thus a home in ancient Greece was simple, dignified, pleasantly proportioned, and sparsely furnished. But contrary to the popular impression, the Greeks didn't live in a bleached white environment any more than they spent all day reading Aristotle. Like other Mediterranean peoples, they used color freely—in frescoes, rugs, decorative painting on furniture, vases, and so on.

By comparison, in eighteenth-century France, furnishings were designed primarily for the aristocracy and nobility and reflect their values. The dominant theme is extravagant and perishable luxury: hand-carved moldings of gold leaf, silk brocade upholstery, graceful, delicate furniture. Indeed the furniture was so fragile, much of it isn't here any more. It wasn't built to last (durability is a bourgeois concern). Labor was cheap and provided prized decorative features, including elaborate handmade veneers and inlays. Machinery was still a curiosity, used in fabulous clockwork toys. Apart from gold, the most popular colors were impractical whites and pastels. Generally, there still wasn't a great deal of furniture, even in the richest homes, and almost none at all in poor homes. Furniture was still produced a piece at a time.

Nineteenth-century English furnishings reflect the success of the Industrial Revolution and the rise of the middle class. Most furniture was machine-made, solid, heavy, and serious. It was turned out in quantity, and those who could afford to bought in quantity. Clutter became a status symbol. Unmusical families not only owned a piano and a harp (among other instruments) but had a special music room as well. Wealthy homes couldn't function without servants—just keeping everything dusted and polished was a full-time job—and there were plenty of poor to fill the role. But the working classes did have more belongings than in the past: proper beds, dishes, chairs, tables, bureaus, and wardrobes.

In the Victorian era, furniture design was a mélange of stolen styles: Gothic, Oriental, French, and so on. This was partly the result of the somewhat unrefined and omnivorous taste of the new middle class, partly the result of an interest in exotic places and the expansion of the Empire, and partly the result of not yet having conceived how machines might be used best and most originally. Just as we still try to make plastic look like wood instead of what it is, the Victorians tended to reproduce old designs with machines, instead of creating new designs suitable for the new style of production. For example, imitations of hand carving were made by having machines gouge out wood (the hollows were then filled with gold leaf).

The most characteristic furniture of the twentieth century is the clean-lined, simple style associated with Bauhaus, Scandinavian, and Italian designers. The emphasis is on function, economy of form, and the quality of the materials. This is appropriate in a culture that depends on efficient machine work and a minimum of handwork.

But, of course, no single style completely characterizes a culture. There are always countercurrents. For instance, at the turn of the century, Art Nouveau challenged industrialism with designs that were elaborate, convoluted, asymmetrical, and organic. They were "natural" in the sense of deriving from natural forms and also in the sense that they could not, theoretically, be made by machines.

In the 1920s, Bauhaus designers created machine-made furniture that definitely looked it. They studied the principles and products of contemporary industry and brought them into the home. This was the most revolutionary and significant movement in modern design, and the fundamental concept was functionalism and economy in design ("Form follows function." "Less is more"). The Bauhaus artists worked primarily with clean, durable materials—glass, steel, chrome, leather. Their work was nonorganic and nondecorative.

In the thirties, in the face of the worldwide Depression the Art Deco movement reacted against minimum design, severity, and asceticism. The inspiration was urban (sometimes Hollywood) sophistication. The emphasis was on large-scale luxury, color, and decoration (primarily in geometric patterns). Industrial materials (glass, plastic, chrome) were used but in ways that suggest a boudoir or cocktail lounge rather than a factory or office. For example, distinctive Art Deco elements are fabulous mirrors, plastic insets on furniture, chrome detailing.

After the war, the world was tired from the years of full-blast production and military regimentation. Led by Scandinavian designers, there was a return to natural, warmer colors and materials, especially teak and walnut. The stress was again on undecorated, but not hard-edged, simplicity. As translated in the mass market, this began to mean unalleviated blandness. By contrast, today's Italian designers have introduced more intense colors and (once again) industrial materials well adapted to machine work. They're noted especially for fine designs in plastic.

Each movement has contributed something valuable. I feel that by now we should recognize that industrial materials are here to stay, they function well, and they can be beautiful. However, we do need comfort, a little Victorian overstuffedness, some suggestion of nature, and some decoration and luxurious color.

The best concepts of the best designers have only had a moderate influence on actual homes. Looking at the entire range of furnishings in America, I'd have to say that sheer quantity of possessions is still accepted as a symbol of respectability and success. And we don't seem to be entirely comfortable with our contemporary identity; for the most successful lines of furniture are those imitating furniture from another time and, often, another place.

Actually, many people aren't fully aware that they always buy a certain *kind* of furniture, and they find it odd if you ask them about it. What they buy is regular furniture. Other kinds of furniture are offbeat. Given this frame of mind, it's extremely difficult to bring any significant new ideas into the home.

By far the most successful furniture style is "traditional" and its variations, all the way from good antiques to garish bastardizations. The middle ground in this range is occupied by what I call "standard imitation traditional," which includes the most successful furniture lines of all: the so-called French provincial, Italian provincial, Early American and colonial, Spanish, Mediterranean, and Renaissance. This kind of furniture is in so many homes that it's come to typify homeyness.

In reality, traditional furniture isn't at all traditional, and in detail and materials it doesn't even qualify as a first-rate copy. The designs are evolved (or copied from competitors) in industry centers (notably High Point, North Carolina) on the basis of what

Modular furniture of my own design.

sold well last year. Decorative motifs, such as "carved" rosettes, are borrowed from the most popular styles, with no historical sense of what the original furniture was like.

What you get, then, is a design "theme."

The more expensive pieces are usually fairly solidly put together, although they're often not as comfortable or as practical as they could be (for example, the upholstery could be easier to maintain and replace).

This kind of mass-produced furniture is packaged in lines, and the lines are tied in with other products. The basic unit in a line is the set (living room, dining room, bedroom, etc.). Sets began to come in during the Victorian era and are now, unfortunately, well established. A typical living room set has a sofa, a coffee table, two end tables, two chairs—all with matching legs from the same mold.

From the consumer's point of view, it's almost never smart (in either sense of the word) to buy furniture in sets. You can generally get better quality for your money by buying a piece at a time. The pieces in a set all match, which is supposed to create a finished, "decorator's" look. But as often as not what it creates is a boring look. Matching is greatly overvalued and ties you into a total take-it-or-leave-it arrangement. A home furnished with individually selected pieces is much more flexible in the directions it can change, and it can change more gradually.

Furniture lines are tied in with the lamp and accessory markets. To go with Spanish provincial, there are decorative figurines (for example, wire statuettes of Don Quixote), gigantic wooden spoons, and Spanishy rugs. For French provincial, there are gold-painted candle sconces and clocks to match, columned

lamps, and do-it-yourself antiquing kits. For Early American, there are spinning-wheel lamps, milk-can umbrella stands, eagle door knockers, even fake dowels on the refrigerator and a "Revolutionary" cabinet for the stereo and TV. We all know George Washington didn't watch TV, so who's fooling whom? What's wrong with a TV set that looks as if it was made in the twentieth century? (The simplicity of some of the Japanese designs for electronic equipment compares very favorably with work that's fancied up to look traditional.)

Finally, the furniture and accessories are tied in with wallpapers and matching fabrics.

Most customers aren't aware how they're being manipulated in their purchases. Once a person is committed to a couple of large pieces of furniture or a few rolls of paper, it's easy to sell him items that are intended to go with what he's got. It's a hard pitch to resist. No one wants things that *don't* go together.

What makes me most unhappy is when young people fall into this trap. I've seen so many start with the idea of doing something special and then end up with the same tired furniture sets their parents had or, worse, poorly made versions of the sets their parents had.

Traditional-type furniture is often kept for many, many years, and it is always as dull and anonymous as the day it was bought. The homeyness it conveys is soap-opera homeyness—bland, impersonal, and claustrophobic.

At the vulgar end of the spectrum of traditional furniture is "gaudy traditional." This wonderful stuff is bought mainly by the new rich and the upper lower class. In my experience the most fabulous collections of gaudy furniture are found in Texas. But no matter what state you're in, when you see a twelve-foot rose-and-white brocade sofa in a suburban ranch house, you're in the presence of true gaudy traditional. The style is characterized by huge, fancy lamps reaching almost to the ceiling; vast, unwieldy draperies, with heavy fringes and tassels, and topped by monstrous valences; ornate gilded mirrors and picture frames (containing nineteenth-century-type academic or impressionist paintings); marble tables and marble statues (sometimes real, sometimes plaster of Paris); fake fireplaces; lots of crystal, especially rococo chandeliers; porcelain figurines; heavy fabrics, such as brocades, damasks, and velvets (usually patterned); and wall-to-wall carpets with a pile four inches deep. As a rule, gold and white are the dominant colors, followed by dark red and purple, which suggest palaces, of course.

In gaudy homes the main rooms usually aren't used very much. I know one home where there's a separate living room, kitchen, and dining room just for guests. In many gaudy homes, including expensive ones, the furniture is protected with plastic.

Owners of gaudy furniture want to appear incredibly rich and successful, and some of them are. Certainly they spend a lot on their furniture.

Utterly different from the gaudy style is the "conservative" market, which consists of costly, accurate copies of antiques and neutral modernish furniture, such as the plain oblong sofa upholstered in a sensible fabric, the unmemorable, substantial lounge chair. Conservative furniture is bought by well-to-do conservative people who insist on good value. But I have my doubts about the sense of spending a lot of money for reproductions. In the end a good copy is still just a copy.

This reasoning is also put forward by those who furnish their homes with genuine antiques. These homes cluster in the older towns and cities (Boston, New York, Philadelphia, Richmond, Charleston, Atlanta, New Orleans, Chicago, San Francisco). Some of the owners do come from old wealth; others pretend they do. Their collections are highly respectable and uncontroversial (which today means primarily English furniture). Their country homes are, typically, Early American. The ambience is quiet and attractive, the quality of the furniture ranges from good to superb. But these homes have little of the passion and idiosyncrasy that characterize great collections. Rather, they feature model, authentic, careful rooms that may be almost of museum quality but contain no surprises or excitement. (I'm talking here about the best of the antiquers, not those who pick up items here and there at flea markets, and whose homes are usually a hodgepodge but sometimes very appealing.)

I do respect what the buyers of antiques are doing to preserve the furniture of the past, but still their homes seem to me uncomfortable physically and emotionally. It's not just that antique furniture is usually frail, rickety, and hard to maintain. It would be impossible to live comfortably today in an eighteenth- or nineteenth-century home, even if the furniture were in mint condition. We can learn from the past but we can't live in it. We aren't eighteenth-century people, and in countless ways we have different needs. We're physically bigger. Our clothing is different (which affects, for example, comfort in seating). Our children are usually around the house, not in a nursery or boarding school. Many women work; few have a household staff. Our entertaining is less formal. And so on.

137

We can't change our true heritage. We can borrow from the past. We can create a sense of the past. But not all the authenticity in the world is going to recreate the past. And so what? Even if you could, would you really be willing to give up electric lights, the telephone, and air conditioners?

A livelier approach to furnishing is the mix-and-match (mostly match) style. If you read decorating magazines or women's magazines, you've seen thousands of examples of this, some fairly attractive, some grotesque. The common denominator is that the space is dominated by colors and patterns. The main idea is to create rooms that will thrill guests when you show them around.

So what's wrong with that? Isn't it nice to be colorful? Not if the riot of color has no relationship to the functions of the space, to the needs of the people in it. Not if the color is just too much to take. A home that knocks your eye out is a great advertisement for the decorator. Unfortunately, having your eye knocked out isn't so much fun on an everyday basis.

Many designers inherit clients who've had a bad experience with another designer. A number of my clients have had troubles with the mixing and matching decorators. A danger sign is the arrival of rolls and rolls of wallpaper and yards and yards of fabric for places you hadn't thought you needed fabric, e.g., on your bed as a little skirt, or over tables and bureaus as drapes. (One fabric fanatic even asked me to upholster her fiberglass planters.) Two other warning signs are a mania for exact color matches and for matching design motifs, such as brass nailheads everywhere. Finally, mixers and

matchers have a weakness for "in" colors. A few years ago acid green was it. Unforgettable.

Mix-and-match was created by decorators and, I'd say, for decorators. But since it's been so widely publicized, it's become widely popular. Unfortunately, the style is all on the surface, and when everything in a home is so artificially coordinated and matched, the people who live there start looking artificial, too.

If you can't stand frills and patterns, you may be tempted by the Bauhaus style or the latest version of it. Everthing is very precise and cold, and you've seen it a thousand times. Exactly in the middle of the entertainment space is a low sofa, two Barcelona chairs, and a Mies coffee table. The dining area features four Breuer chairs around a butcher-block-type table (for warmth).

The Bauhaus movement was exciting in its time when people needed to become aware they were living in a new age with an aesthetic of its own. But after so many decades, the Bauhaus doesn't have to be taken quite so seriously and wholeheartedly. No one's afraid of glass and chrome anymore. Mies van der Rohe's Barcelona chair looks fine in the Museum of Modern Art and has become an enduring status symbol. But is it comfortable? I feel that it holds you in one position and is hard to get out of.

The Bauhaus artists deserve gratitude for cleaning out of many people's minds and homes the endless shelves of trivia, smothering yards of heavy fabric, and overbearing, gloomy furniture. But the Bauhaus style also pushed out comfort and color, fantasies and hobbies. And people who live in a Bauhaus environment seem more cold and compulsive than they really are.

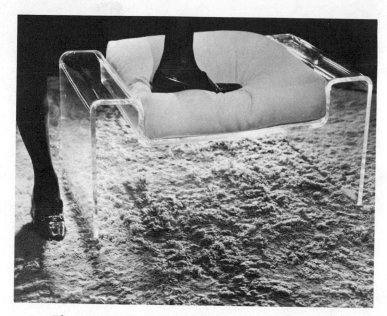

Plastic is tough and versatile. This can be a footrest, table or seat.

Very different from the preceding groups are the trendy pacesetters, the excitable butterflies of the decorating world, who change their life-styles and their homes every year and a half. One season out go the tiger skin rugs and in come supergraphics; next year out go the supergraphics, in come corrugated aluminum walls. Pacesetters are fun, but there's seldom any sense or substance behind the style. They pay a high price for confusion.

Finally there are people who just don't care about their surroundings. Some live most of their lives in hotels. Others buy suites of furniture without thought and keep them until they wear out completely. These people live in drab ugliness without ever seeming to care. Some of them are simply drifters. Some have never experienced anything better. A few are successful and educated but fanatically involved in work. Whatever the cause, the situation is sad. Everyone needs a home.

We all belong to some social group and have picked up social habits without thinking about them. It's important to step aside occasionally from the social role you're playing and the setting you've created for it. Are you really living the way you want to live?

Take a critical look at each piece of furniture you own with a few questions in mind: Do I need it? What for? What does it do for me, and does it do it economically, that is, as simply as possible? Is the size appropriate and convenient? Is it durable? Is it easy to clean and maintain? Is it easy to move?

The living room sofa is typically a large, heavy, and expensive piece of furniture. Some of the size

Modular furniture of my own design.

is usually wasted, because it's almost never used by three people despite the three seats. It is difficult to move for cleaning and even more difficult to move to a new home. And in a new home it may not fit where you need it. A large sofa is a heavy visual element that's difficult to balance. And finally, an upholstered sofa is hard to clean and very costly to redo.

If you want a sofa primarily as seating for guests, consider some alternatives. Your basic problem is to find the nicest places to sit, with the most interesting views, and then to find appropriate seating. You need furniture that's proportional to the space and is flexible. People aren't going to want to sit in the same arrangement on all occasions. And you may want to change your gathering places according to the season—for instance, it's nice to be around a fire in winter, near a window in spring.

Alternatives to the sofa include banquettes against one or more walls (or angled into the center of the space); a modified, or platform, sofa; modular seating; or simply a comfortable variety of chairs, benches, pouffes. For all lounge furniture, always consider having cushioning covered with removable slipcovers instead of upholstery. When a cover wears out, the old one can be the pattern for the new one, and you can have different covers for different seasons. It's nice to sit on velvet in winter, but cotton is better in summer.

The advantage of banquettes you design yourself is that they're usually simpler, more elegant, and more attractive than mass-produced seating, and often better constructed. The proportions can be tailored to your space. Banquettes can be built to make use of corners or other spaces likely to be wasted. If they're to be used for private relaxation, they can

141

be built into out-of-the-way spots. And they're relatively inexpensive. If you're not up to carpentry yourself, it should be easy to find someone to build the platform, and you can buy the cushions and fabric from an upholsterer.

Modular units are available in all styles and colors, including many good contemporary designs. They can be bought a piece at a time, which helps a budget and also prevents your getting locked into a style before you're sure about it. They are, of course, the ultimate in flexibility.

I have five large modified sofas in my entertainment space. Two of us built them over a weekend. This kind of seating is right for parties where there's a lot of movement. Traffic flows freely around and through the area. The seating doesn't polarize or compartmentalize a space the way a sofa does with its clearly defined back and sides. And finally, my setup is inexpensive and easy to maintain.

Most homes have too many tables of the wrong kind. I've made the point about dining room tables. They can be terrible space-wasters. But other tables have their problems as well.

There are three possible functions for a table. To keep things in, to keep things on, to work on. Many tables don't adequately perform any of these functions. If your home is short of space, each table should, ideally, perform all these functions.

Do you know what's in your table drawers? Do you need it? Are these drawers the most convenient place to store whatever it is?

Too often tables have small and/or sticky drawers or, sometimes, deep cavernous drawers. Think twice about a table you feel you need for stor-

The modular seating in my entertainment space.

age purposes; the chances are it provides little storage space relative to its total size.

What's on top of your tables? Many tables hold only a lamp and perhaps some bric-a-brac or a magazine. Certainly you don't need a table just to hold a lamp when there are floor lamps, pole lamps, wall lights, and overheads. Bric-a-brac can probably be better displayed elsewhere—on a mantle, on a shelf, or in a case—if it's worth displaying. Magazines can always go in a magazine rack.

End tables near sofas sometimes hold not only a lamp and an *objet* or two, but also an ashtray and a couple of books and magazines, and perhaps nuts and candy. The trouble with these tables is they're hard to reach, being somewhat behind a person seated on the sofa. Items that are going to be reached for regularly are better placed on a coffee table or on one or two other tables in front of the seating.

Don't get a dainty little table if what you need is a good big one. If you like to put your feet up, or your friends do, get a table that can take this treatment. Or put a small table slightly to one side, and have a stool, bench, or bolster for your feet.

Flowers and plants are nice on tables, but they're also nice in large vases or planters on the floor, hanging from the ceiling, on shelves, or even on a pedestal.

Beware of low, little tables that don't hold much but catch you in the shins, and hall tables that get in the way and attract clutter.

Bedside tables present some of the same problems as sofa-side tables, only worse: They're hard to reach and things get knocked over. Also, they're typically too small, with one tiny drawer for all the things one needs, sometimes quickly and in the dark.

A mattress on a platform is much less expensive than the traditional bed with bedside tables.

144

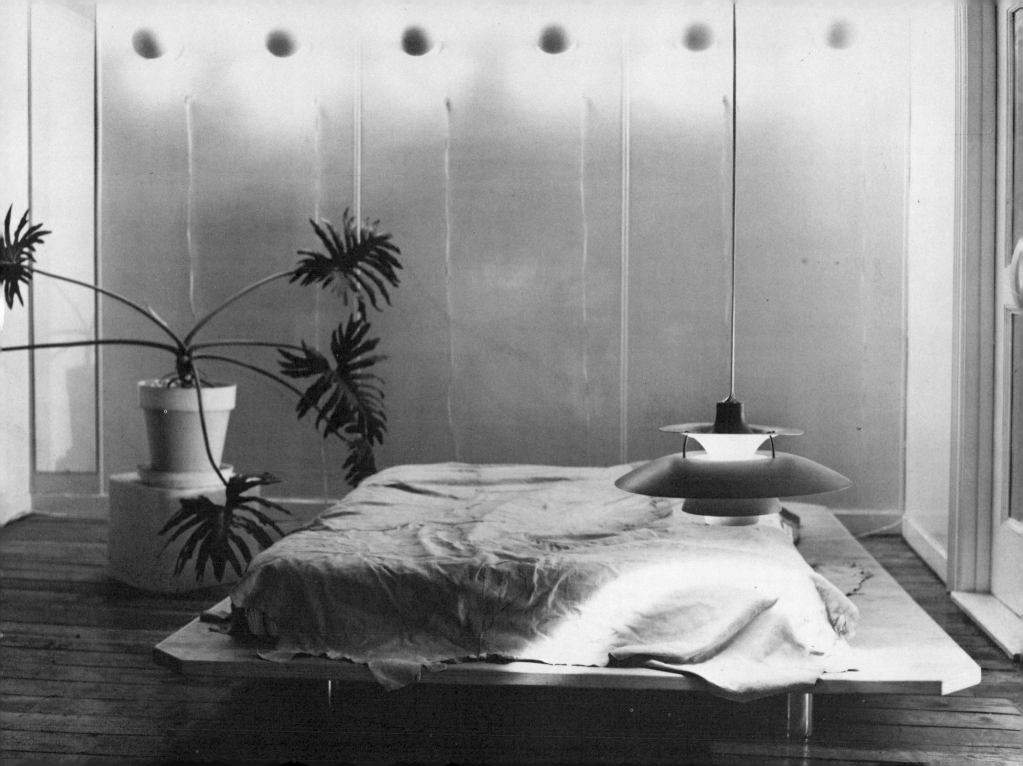

Maybe you've seen a standard bedside table and drawer holding a clock-radio, telephone, reading light, Kleenex, pills, contraceptive, books, hairbrush, whiskey glass, smoking paraphernalia, and ashtray. It's not a beautiful sight, and there's no room left for some of the other things that might be nice to have by the bed: perhaps a couple of plants, a hair dryer, a small TV, switches for the stereo and the room lights.

There's no single design that can replace the conventional bedside table, because each person's needs are different. But there are a few principles that usually apply. (1) More surface area is needed, whether a single surface, shelves, or whatever. (2) Items you pick up frequently should be kept low and to the side. (3) The reading light should be above and behind you. (4) Switches for lights, radio, TV, etc., can be behind the head. (5) Items used infrequently can also be behind the head or on shelves or in drawers under the bed.

A simple solution that's some help is to put a low table on each side of the bed, extending about a third of the way down. You can also semienclose the bed with shelving at the head, which provides not only a snug feeling but better storage. Or you can completely enclose the bed. It's possible to buy enclosed bed units containing telephone, plants, and storage space. But ideally the bed area should be custom-made from your design for you, according to your plan of what you want where. (Remember to consider linen storage.)

You don't need permanent table or seating space for guests at your parties. Instead you can use nesting, folding, or multipurpose tables. There are several varieties of tables that can be disassembled and some-

times used for multiple purposes. For example, I've designed a clear acrylic sculptured chair that when turned on its side becomes a table base. I have clients who are artists, and they use these chairs in their home gallery. When they have a large number of people in for a showing, they usually serve hors d'oeuvres on a twelve-foot-long table made of the chairs turned on their sides and three forty-eight-inch square pieces of glass that are ordinarily stored in a closet. There are also rectangular table bases (by Tri-Mark in Philadelphia) that make a coffee table when placed on their sides and a dining table when placed on end. And I have a friend who uses fiber glass planters for table bases when she's entertaining a large group.

In a small area, fold-up tables that fold against a wall or into a wall cabinet are often extremely useful as extra kitchen counter space, for informal eating, as an occasional desk, or for hobbies and games. These are available commercially in several different styles.

Bureaus are bulky, overvalued items. The drawers are almost never really convenient. If there's a mirror it's probably too far back and is too poorly lit to be useful (and anyway only reflects the upper half of you). The top of the bureau tends to get covered with things you don't have a place for or you've never got around to putting away: sewing to be done, hairbrush, lotions, rollers, magazines, costume jewelry, and so on, or briefcase, stray socks, cuff links, comb, magazines, and so on.

I avoid bureaus and build shelves or cabinets instead. There are also plastic shelf units that are inexpensive and readily available in a number of different colors.

The king-size bed is another problematic piece

of furniture. These beds are so fashionable, they're stuffed into small bedrooms, leaving no space for dressing, doing exercises, or even walking around. I gave up a client recently because she wanted me to redesign her bedroom, which was entirely filled with a bed. She was all of ninety-five pounds. I tried to explain that a king-size bed wasn't necessary to her happiness, and that there was nothing I could do with the room, unless she got a smaller bed.

Honestly, there's nothing wrong with a queen-size bed or a standard double. I've even heard of people who sleep on single beds. And I've *never* heard of a potential lover going back home because the bed was too small.

When I was a child everyone had a standard double. Then twin singles became popular (probably thanks to the movies—it was taboo to show two people, married or not, in the same bed). Then the twin singles were pushed together—a great step. Then queen-size and king-size took over. I think it's time to get back to the standard double, especially when the bedroom space is limited.

I'm not a fan of gimmicky beds. Round beds are nice to look at but often not practical. They take up more space relative to the sleeping area, and you're apt to find yourself falling off them. If you're Jean Harlow material, maybe you need one. If you're not, maybe you don't. (A round bed in a round room, though, is something else.)

Hospital-type beds that can be moved into different positions are very convenient for reading and television. And it's healthy to get your feet up. These beds are expensive, but may be well worth it if you spend a lot of time in bed.

For myself I prefer an innerspring mattress on a platform. I used to have the platform about twelve inches off the floor but found I had a hard time getting onto my feet in the morning. So now I have the platform thirty-six inches high, and in the morning I fall out on my feet, with no choice but to proceed with another day.

Giant TV sets are as common as giant beds, and I just as often wonder why. The smaller the screen, the tighter the picture, and the closer you can sit to it without losing clarity. You have to sit far back from a large set for a clear picture, and often there just isn't room to get that far away. Select the appropriate size TV for the distance at which it will be viewed. You shouldn't have to look up or down to see the screen, so the standard cabinet arrangement is usually too low. If you usually watch television while lying on a sofa or in bed, then the best placement may be rather high, even suspended from the ceiling. Get the most practical setup and forget about those fancy coffin-shaped cabinets. They belong underground.

Whenever possible I substitute portable sets for the big-brother family model. When everyone gathers around the TV, the result is more often fights than togetherness. Even if you're living alone, it may be more convenient to have a set that follows you, instead of you going to it.

Sometimes people don't arrange for comfortable viewing, because they don't like to admit they do view. Be honest. Even if you only look at the thing once in a while, do it right.

I have a client who loves to watch sports. I've built him a home amphitheater around a video beam for the ultimate in TV luxury, with a videotape system so he can see later a game he's missed. I've heard

147

An amphitheater for TV viewing. The projector in the photo on the left throws the image on the screen shown in the photo on the right.

of people flying all the way to Miami to watch the Super Bowl on a TV set in a hotel. I don't pretend to understand this. But I acknowledge it.

Some people, including quite a few decorators, feel a living room without a grand (or at least baby grand) piano isn't complete. I'm not talking about people who are music lovers. The piano's for show. Usually the explanation is that it's for the children (who play the electric guitar, if anything) or for parties (at which pianists never appear). The cleaning woman keeps the instrument polished, and the top's usually propped up as if someone's about to sit down and run through some Rachmaninoff.

I wouldn't ever want to call a musical instrument ugly, but a big piano is certainly big—and heavy and very black. It's fine in a concert hall, but the only reason to have one in a home is if it's really played and loved. Otherwise it's a pretentious embarrassment.

For most parties and most players a good upright is entirely adequate. When a child is learning to play, renting may be preferable to buying. When a substantial investment is made in the instrument, the pressure on the child is often too great: "We bought you the Steinway, *now you play it.*" This is not the spirit for creating a musician.

Other prized status symbols include breakfronts, étagères, armoires, and other old-fashioned, inefficient pieces of furniture, frequently with drawers or doors that have to be pulled gently with a little key and tassel.

The giant breakfront is one of the conventional standbys of traditional furniture. It's generally way out of proportion to contemporary homes, but its popularity mysteriously increases. I like a fine break-

front in the right surroundings, but they belong in older homes, with high ceilings and spacious rooms, not in small apartments and ranch houses.

A breakfront is supposed to add weight and character to a room; for example, in a living room that doesn't have a fireplace, sometimes a breakfront is used as a substitute focus of interest. But too often it just adds weight.

The drawers of a breakfront are generally sticky and full of lost things: batteries, coasters, loose photographs, decks of cards, pencils, napkins. The display shelves are typically dark and contain bric-a-brac.

Etagères of various sorts are also used for bric-a-brac and other treasures. The étagère was originally a French concept and is essentially a curio cabinet without the glass and doors. In recent years decorators began using the term, the idea got back to manufacturers, and now you can buy an étagère in any style from imitation French provincial to steel and glass modern, for from $19.95 to $1,995.

The idea of having a special place for things you value is fine. It's not fine when you buy an étagère because there's a blank space against a wall, and then you go out shopping for things to put in the étagère. Etagères are sometimes sold as room dividers, but usually they're too flimsy for this purpose.

As for armoires, why are they needed in a home with good closets? Typically, in an armoire the rod is too high, the interior is too dark, shallow, and confining. And they're extremely bulky. (The space in an armoire can sometimes be put to better use by building in shelving.)

The armoire is another example of a status symbol that's bought with good intentions but for effect—usually as an interesting way to fill a void. I feel this is a big price to pay for decoration, in more ways than one.

Many decorators rely on one or two period pieces per room, such as an armoire or breakfront, to set a "theme." But a room that has a purpose can do without a theme.

While you're throwing away, look around for dilapidated furniture. It's often found in dens and children's rooms: chairs with springs popping out and cushions sliding onto the floor, shaky tables, stained rugs, sagging beds, rotting upholstery, and so on. A lived-in look is heartwarming, but a broken-down look is depressing. And the family deserves at least as good as the guests. Grungy furniture can often be fixed up, with paint or slipcovers or minor repairs. But if it's had it, get rid of it.

Once you start looking at furniture critically and in terms of function, you start making design judgments, although you may not be aware of it. Effective function is fundamental to good design.

Furniture shouldn't be confused with art. Furniture is meant to be used, and no matter how beautiful it is, if it isn't comfortable, sturdy, durable, etc., it's not good furniture.

In the traditional concept of aesthetically good design, the relevant factors are material or texture, mass, line, and sometimes color. These elements must be put into a harmonious, balanced relationship. Perhaps the most subtle quality is line. In imitations of fine furniture, whether of an Adam secretary or a Saarinen table, the line is apt to be wrong. A curve has been slightly flattened or an angle has been slightly closed, and the imitation is not quite as beautiful as the original, although you may not be able to

see immediately where the problem is. However, even here practical considerations play a role. Monkeying with the line can affect the stability of a table or the comfort of a chair. If you're satisfied with the practical aspects of a piece of furniture, it's probably aesthetically well-made, too.

If you have a sense of fun, fantasy, and humor, you can express this in your furniture. Personally, I can't live deadpan all the time. Among my own designs, I have a chair that looks like a lady's shoe, a luncheonette booth, and pouffes in the shapes of hearts and stars.

If there is one principle that can help to sort out the variables in achieving good design, it's to choose simplicity over complexity: furniture with clean lines, rooms with only one or two bright colors, uncluttered space, plain fabrics. If you feel in the end the results are too severe, it's easy to introduce more color and curlicues.

Incidentally, one feature many people never consider in terms of simplicity versus complexity is what Eero Saarinen called the "ugly and confusing, unrestful world" of chair and table legs. Low legs, no legs, or pedestal bases can do a lot to clear up the problem.

You'd think simple furniture would be cheaper and easier to find than gimmicked stuff, but it isn't. As I've said, making your own furniture or having it made for you is often the best solution.

The easiest kind of furniture to make is tables. A table is just a top on legs or a base, or a single unit, such as a plastic cube, a tree trunk, or the like. The top can be wood, glass, plastic laminate, marble, cork, slate, a hollow-core door (which is light), or just about anything. The supports can be sawhorses,

151

plywood cubes, heavy construction pipe, electric wire spools, crates, or ready-made legs, which are available in many varieties of styles. A table doesn't have to be expensive to be elegant. For example, the *New York Times* did an article on jewelry designer Elsa Peretti's apartment in New York, and the occasional tables (including coffee tables) are made from bleached and sanded packing crates.

Apart from furniture you make yourself, you're most apt to find well-made and well-designed furniture at the decorators' marts. These stores depend on a large volume of return business for their success. If their products are unsatisfactory, they're in trouble. Of course, the problem is that nonprofessionals can't buy in these stores. You need to have someone from the trade make the purchases for you. However, you usually can examine the merchandise and ask the retail price. When you have an idea of what you want, then you can make arrangements with a decorator.

You can also find good furnishings at a good department store. The trick is to pick out the superior pieces from the mass of mediocre ones.

It's amusing to shop at the Salvation Army and other thrift stores. In fact, I know people who go out and buy beat-up old furniture when they have better beat-up old furniture at home they could restore. But even though they're fun, the flea markets and thrift stores are usually better sources for accessories than for basic furniture. In order to get good value, you not only have to understand furniture quite well, you have to be able to get to the stores early on the days deliveries are made. In Atlanta, The Flea Market (a store) unloads a forty-foot van full of furniture, lamps, and accessories every six weeks. I've seen women disassemble tables and

A shoe chair for the boudoir.

Furniture doesn't have to be serious.

lamps while fighting over them. Find out when deliveries come in at your local (reliable) used-furniture shop, and you'll probably find a better selection than at the more famous outlets.

The United States is evidently jammed full of people who know at least a little about old furniture and are out scouting for it. It's a seller's market, and for every shopper with an eagle eye who finds bargains, there are a hundred who pay too much and end up with junk.

You can get a chest of drawers for forty dollars, but by the time it's refinished, the drawers are waxed, the joints are glued, and the hardware replaced, a bargain can turn into a trauma. (Incidentally, never believe it if you're told that a bit of hardware will be easy to find.)

Secondhand upholstered pieces are especially treacherous. A $75 sofa can end up costing $400 plus fabric after you've replaced the webbing and the springs and had the frame reglued.

On the other hand, simple chairs and tables can be a good buy at thrift shops. They're often basically better made than contemporary versions, and for an informal situation, where a fresh coat of paint is as good as a new finish, they can be just right.

I understand the appeal of bargain hunting, and some of my favorite things have come from flea markets, but too much of anything is too much. It's fashionable to buy used furniture, for obvious reasons: There's a great variety, it's inexpensive, and you can fill up spaces faster and easier. But your home can also end up looking like a used-furniture store.

Whether you're buying new or old, if an item has drawers, they're often the best indication of how well it's made. One of the limitations on home-made furniture is that it's hardly worthwhile to build anything with drawers unless you're seriously into carpentry. They're too difficult.

Drawers, of course, should pull in and out smoothly. Many new drawers are on steel tracks, which are slick, and so there must be stops that work or the whole drawer will slide out in your hands.

In contemporary designs there are often gimmicky drawer arrangements. Be sure the system works. If you can't pull open each drawer easily with one hand, don't get the piece. Also, check the handles. Many are made of thin plastic that breaks readily.

If, when you open a drawer, you move or jostle the piece of furniture, you probably shouldn't buy it. This can happen with the latest plastic designs or with some of the world's most expensive antiques. It means the piece of furniture is either very light or unbalanced.

Many people don't worry about the construction of everyday chairs, although they're careful to get well-built lounge chairs. Actually, everyday chairs take much more of a beating and have to be much sturdier. They're pushed and pulled back and forth by whoever's sitting in them, tilted onto their back legs, used as stepladders, sat in backwards, and so on.

If you're thinking of buying a chair, take it by the back and give it a good bounce on its two back legs. There shouldn't be any give. Sit in it and pull it back and forth as if you were sitting down to a table; tilt it back. You shouldn't feel the joints giving under the stress.

There are some lovely, graceful chairs around that aren't comfortable and don't last. Some of the knock-offs of bentwood chairs aren't good for much more than six months, and they can be agony if you

A combination of traditional and modern motifs. Not very serious but very comfortable. (My own design.)

155

have to sit on one for, say, an entire dinner. Rattan work also doesn't last well unless it's been done by hand, not set in the frame. (If it's done by hand, you'll know by the price.)

The butt-and-back test is all important in chair buying. Sit in the chair. It should feel good. The back of the chair should support the lower part of your back. You should be able to sit all the way back and straight up, turned to one side with your legs crossed, or in whatever positions you're apt to wiggle into in normal use of the chair. Generally the seat has to be upholstered or cushioned to be comfortable, but if it's well carved or molded, then even plain wood or plastic chairs are fine. Director's chairs are also good if sturdy and made so that your back is supported at the right place.

The back of a chair shouldn't be straight, but on an angle. A straight back will make you feel you're being pushed forward.

For everyday chairs, I often do recommend getting old ones. They're typically made of thicker wood, reinforced with dowels and stretchers, with good, angled backs. I look for old office chairs, cruise chairs, or the dinette-set type.

A good inexpensive source for new chairs can be restaurant suppliers. Every large city has a restaurant-supply section, and you'd be amazed at the interesting designs available, even old café chairs.

If you're buying new lounge chairs, a sofa, or the like, you usually can count on the structure to stand up to average use (if it's from a reliable store). But sometimes the legs are joined on too flimsily. See if the piece of furniture is movable, and if it is, whether the legs move with it. Also, check the fabric. If it has a loose weave (if you can see the weave from

I designed this coffee table of clear acrylic, which can also be used as a side table.

156

158

three feet away), it's apt to wear out more quickly than you'd like. And if the fabric is pulled too tightly over the wood, it will wear out at the stress points.

Sit on lounge furniture and bounce. If there is a depression you sink into (which should happen only with something secondhand), then the springs are giving way. You shouldn't have any awareness of springs at all. The padding should be consistently firm throughout, and I just don't think you can make padding that's *too* thick or *too* comfortable. If there are cushions, remove them and test the condition of the underlying springs by pressing down with your hand. There shouldn't be sags or bulges. Examine the cushions. They shouldn't be lumpy or limp.

With modern plastic furniture, I have to warn that some appealing designs are made too light in weight. There are some modular cubes with drawers that look fine, but the drawers slide right out, and stacking is impractical because the units slide and topple too easily. And very lightweight plastic furniture is often brittle and fragile, and if it breaks it can't be properly repaired.

Many people object to clear acrylic furniture because it scratches; however, I don't feel this is a drawback. Over time, ordinary wear creates a fine web of scratches, a patina that actually enhances the piece, much like the scratches on an old refectory table.

Back in 1968, I designed and manufactured acrylic furniture, and today I still love and live with some of my prototypes. The pieces have been moved and moved and really used. I'm happy to say that they look better as time goes on.

I had one very deep scratch on my coffee table which I removed with jeweler's rouge and a buffing

159

wheel. For this, the wheel has to be applied slowly so it doesn't overheat the plastic. For general care I recommend Johnson's "J" wax, which produces a nice hard surface. There are numerous antistatic solutions availabe at plastic supply and fabricating companies.

Clear acrylic furniture was first made in the Art Deco period and was revived in the late 1960s. The beauty of this material is its transparency, strength, and ability to heat-bend to produce soft-looking rounded corners.

Another good, modern material is fiber glass, which is incredibly strong, light, and moldable, and doesn't warp. As for durability, it's used in boats and aircraft where the demands are usually more severe than in the home—even in the children's room. It should be maintained with wax.

Metal has a completely different character from plastic (although you may have some similar scratching problems). Polished or brushed stainless steel is a beautiful and strong metal. It's also expensive. Chrome is a popular substitute and should stand up equally well. But a chrome finish is applied by dipping, and if it's not thick enough it may scratch and chip easily. This also occurs if the underlying metal is too flexible. If you can flake off a bit of chrome with your thumbnail (bends and joints are the most vulnerable places), then the chrome finish is no good. Check out the pieces that have been on display. The chrome should not be marred.

Stainless steel is in my opinion somewhat warmer in tone than chrome, which is usually distinctly cool. Scratches on steel are less of a worry, because the steel can be repolished or rebrushed if necessary. And stainless steel doesn't rust.

Plastic is tough and versatile. This can be a footrest, table or seat.

160

Iron is also a good strong material for furniture. Its weight is a problem, and when it's left black it can look even heavier than it is; but it can be painted white, as much fine lawn furniture is. If in your neighborhood you see homes with new wrought-iron gates, fences, and grills, there's probably an ironworker in the vicinity. He may be able to make up for you furniture of your own design or in a traditional design or in a combination of both. In my area the prices compare very well with retail prices.

Brass and copper are warm metals, if the price and upkeep are all right with you. But be sure you know whether you're getting solid or plate—plate wears much less well. If you have any doubt, apply a Brillo pad to an out-of-the-way spot. If the finish comes out silvery, the metal is plate.

Of all the furniture materials, I still feel wood is the most naturally beautiful. Different woods have characterized different eras: olive and cypress in ancient Greece, oak in the Renaissance, walnut for Queen Anne furniture, mahogany for Chippendale, satinwood for Adam. Today we have the choice of woods of all types and from all over the world. And with cross-graining and new, much-improved glues, we can build strong, lovely pieces.

There's much confusion among consumers over what's a good value in fabrics and upholstery materials. Not only are there thousands of different products, but the weave and conditions of use make a big difference. But perhaps an outline of some of the points I keep in mind when making my own selections will help.

Re the leather–vinyl controversy: Good, soft leather is better than vinyl. Tough, stiff leather isn't. Vinyl is cheaper and easier to clean and maintain.

They make vinyl now that "breathes," but it still isn't as comfortable as good leather. Vinyl won't last as long as leather, but how long do you need it for? Are you planning to mention your furniture in your will?

Suède is also nice to live with, but it's not the choice if you're on a budget. For the price of cleaning a suède sofa you can get a new sofa (not in suède, though). Various imitations, suède cloth, are available. When cotton is supplemented with synthetic yarn, I find it cleans better. Ultrasuède is a particularly good imitation and is machine washable, but it's very costly.

For most purposes I favor natural yarns. But blends of natural and synthetic fibers, such as wool and acrylic, horsehair, cotton, and polyester, or silk and polyester are also good. The synthetic yarns are strong, but tend to lack depth. Natural fibers tend to have a better feel but lack strength and are harder to clean.

When choosing fabric, look for a tight weave. Watch out, though, for corduroy, cordless corduroy, velvets, and velveteens. The weave is tight, but wear will show. I use these materials because they're nice, but not if it's very important that the material last a long time. An old-fashioned velvetlike fabric that does last well is mohair velvet.

In searching for unusual fabrics I give most attention to the specialty houses that work with couture designers. Not only do I find a wide range of fabrics, but, surprisingly, I feel I get better value. I use in quantity a wool flannel that's a suiting and coating material, has a strong weave and a good feel; it comes in a good variety of pleasant colors. Another, similar material is a flannel called chinchilla

161

that has a surface of tiny balls, which provides tactile interest but isn't rough.

A beautiful fabric is bouclé of blended wool, which is extraordinarily soft and moderately durable. (Some versions of this material have weaves that are too loose and stretchy.)

For informal situations nothing is better or stronger than a heavy cotton duck, which comes in many colors and is washable.

And if it can be managed, it's delightful to have one place in the home which is luxurious and impractical, and where you treat yourself to satin or silk (damask, taffeta, or moiré).

ART

Almost every home has some art around—even Holiday Inns have art—but how often do you notice it enough to remember it? When you're visiting friends, how often do you make a point of looking again at a particular painting or sculpture you like?

It's better to have no art in a home than art that means nothing to you. A wall doesn't feel bad without a painting on it; it usually doesn't look bad either. Nevertheless, I've been asked thousands of times, "What should I get to go over the sofa? ". . . in the hall?" ". . . in the alcove?", as if I could suggest a brand name. There's only one answer: Buy what you like. But that doesn't mean indulge ignorance. If you have no idea of what artists are trying to do—of what they've done in the past, of what they're doing today—then educate yourself before buying. Find out what art is about. Go to as many museums and art galleries as possible. Go to lectures, and read art books and art reviews. There are no shortcuts and no rules to take the place of experience.

I don't mean there isn't good art and bad art, but there's no way of substituting the taste and values of some expert or authority for your own judgment. A good collection isn't a random assortment of good pieces. It's shaped by the sensitivity and vision of the collector. You have to get involved.

In getting to know art, remember that you're probably not going to be hanging up any Titians or Monets. The best art of the past doesn't come on the market very often, and when it does, of course, only the very rich can afford it.

I still hear people say that they don't like "modern art," and I have trouble believing my ears. In the last twenty years alone, modern art in painting has meant abstract expressionism, pop art, minimal art, op art, conceptual art, realism—and I'm probably missing a few. Within a number of these types, there's a great variety; think of the difference between Franz Kline and Jackson Pollock. And, in addition, there are always interesting artists who aren't following the major trends, such as Chagall, Ben Shahn, Wyeth.

If you're interested in the work of a particular artist, see as much of it as you can. If possible, meet the artist. Not only will this give you the chance to learn more about his or her work, but if you're seriously interested in buying, a personal relationship can be an advantage.

There's hardly a place in America that doesn't have an artist or two within driving distance. And where you find one serious artist, you'll find others. You may not come across a young Rauschenberg right away, but the more you look, the sharper your eye will become.

Art schools and college and university art departments are centers for young talent. Find out when there will be shows you can attend. Ninety percent of what you see will be mediocre, at best. But every now and then you'll encounter a superior artist. And the price is right. You can afford to buy more impulsively, and if your taste changes in a few years, it's not a financial tragedy. Moreover, it's exciting to buy the work of a young artist and you contribute to the creative process.

If you meet an art dealer or gallery owner you like, don't be defensive. Ask questions. Knowledgeable customers usually do ask questions. It's the beginners who insist, "I know what I like."

Dealers are peculiar people. Some are shady, most are sharp. Most of them are also art lovers. If it weren't for dealers, many more fine artists would have been starved into respectable office jobs. Usually, it isn't a curator or critic or art historian who gives a young artist his start, but a dealer who has faith. The curators move in later.

Dealers also educate the taste of their customers. A great dealer like Joseph Duveen can influence the taste of an entire generation, to say nothing of the worldwide art market. A single show, like Sidney Janis's pop art show some fifteen years ago, can change the public's perception of art overnight.

It's smart to get to know a dealer before trusting him completely, but it's also smart to be aware that a good dealer can do a lot for you. It's wise to hold off on major purchases until you know what a dealer's reputation is among his peers and customers. For example, in buying antiquities, forgeries are a major problem; how would your dealer handle a case in which a piece you bought turned out to be a fake? And, of course, beware of fabulous bargains. It's hard to feel sorry for someone stuck with, say, a forgery of Picasso when the price was so low that he must have thought the canvas was stolen.

If you find a dealer who is sensitive to your tastes, who can expand your art experience, and who finds you art you enjoy, stick with him. This is the relationship that should exist between dealer and customer.

If you're interested in contemporary art but are insecure about your judgment, try to find out what artists and art critics think of the gallery where you're shopping. Is it one they respect? One they'd like to show in? Are the shows reviewed in art periodicals, or in any major newspapers or magazines? Are the gallery's artists being acquired by any important museums? A gallery with a reputation to protect will not usually sell you junk deliberately.

To find new talent modestly priced, you'll probably have to go outside the art establishment, to small new galleries or directly to art schools. And then you're on your own. Which is one reason customers support the major dealers.

The most common worries expressed by the unsophisticated art buyer are: Will it go with my décor? Can I live with it? Is it good quality? Will my guests like it?

If your entire home is overdecorated, jumping with colors and patterns, then *no* art will go with your decor. If you've left yourself some neutral space to develop, then there shouldn't be a problem. You can put a Renaissance painting in a contemporary environment or a Picasso in a Louis XV room. The frame is more apt to cause difficulty than the painting itself.

Whether or not you can live with a particular work of art is a much more intelligent concern. I wouldn't want to wake up every morning to *Guernica*, but if I could have it, I'd build a beautiful place for it. Much important art isn't intended for a home environment. The aesthetic and emotional impact may be too violent or too bitter or just too big for comfort. For such pieces you need a space that isn't used all the time—an alcove, a foyer, or the like.

If you're unsure whether you can coexist with a

piece of art you like, the gallery may allow you to lease with an option to buy. Within a month you should know how you get along with it.

As for quality in art, there are no guarantees no matter how much you spend, as witness Huntington Hartford's terrible collection. Some people turn to antiquities or primitive art to avoid the issue of quality. If their choices aren't the best, still their collection will have some historical or anthropological interest. Unfortunately, these are the very areas where forgery and second-rate imitations are the most widespread, and where the amateur is most likely to get burned. Indeed, the experts are frequently fooled.

The graphic arts are very appealing to the collector who isn't rich. A lot of people can afford a lithograph by Miró or Larry Rivers who couldn't afford one of their oils. But again, be on guard and don't immediately believe everything you're told. For example, did you ever wonder how you know that a limited edition has really been limited? I've even heard uneducated customers being misled with regard to basic distinctions between plain copies and "original" prints. Buy from a reputable dealer, and learn as much as possible about how graphics are produced and marketed.

Graphics by unknown artists can be great bargains. You can often find an interesting print for less than it will cost to frame it. And today, photographs are being bought as art, much as posters and prints were bought a few years ago.

A home doesn't have to have art in it. Perhaps you can't afford the art you like best or it isn't appropriate for your home. What art does in a home can also be accomplished by handcrafts and hobbies, collections and curiosities that reflect your experience and vision of life.

A room can be "decorated" with a rug or a flag, or photographs or tin soldiers; with a collection of butterflies or arrowheads, or posters or a neon sign; with ship models, woven ropes, wood carvings, puppets, pinups, masks, or needlepoint samplers; with an aquarium, a terrarium, a doll's house, children's art, collages, pressed flowers, maps; with clocks, barometers, and astrolabes, and so on. If you're alive, you've had experiences that can be reflected in your home. What do you love from your childhood? What are your hobbies? What kind of books do you read? What kind of vacations do you take? Look inside yourself. Look around—not just when you go on a trip, but going to work, going shopping, taking a walk.

If what turns you on is your old teddy bear or the burble of the neon beer sign in your local bar, that can be your art. Someone will find a name for it, "nostalgia" or "camp" or something.

I enjoy creating my own art and accessories. If a space can use, say, a mobile, I think I can make a good one myself. I also think a lot of other people could, too, if they'd just try.

I have a mobile made of an old bent exhaust pipe I found in the street (suspended by wire). Here a wall is decorated with Mylar stretched over a diamond-shaped frame. The material reflects the light and is pleasantly glittery. You don't have to take it seriously, and when you're tired of it, you can move it to another place or out the door, or cover the frame with something else.

For several years now I've been working with

Mylar on a diamond frame reflects light and patterns.

A mop rug.

different kinds of mops for making wall hangings, rugs, and sculptures. I use and sell industrial mops made of rayon, which can be made into "rugs" of the sort shown here. Household mops (the kind you put through a wringer) are softer. I work with a type made of rayon, which is easy to dye.

Using ordinary objects, often junk, as art has again become popular among artists. The idea dates back to the Dadaists, early in the century.

Since the onset of the machine age, we've produced so many different kinds of material things that whole and fragmented pieces of our world are, unfortunately, everywhere. Some of it may look like trash. Some of it may be beautiful. Yesterday's machines are today's art. For example, in the Dakota apartment building, one of the tenants built a bar out of the old mahogany and brass elevator fixtures. And tomorrow, today's machines will have their connoisseurs.

A bent pipe or a piece of driftwood or a rock is neither beautiful or ugly. But you may see how the material's color and shape can be used in a particular space. An artist works with the eyes and the head as much as the hands. I look for objects at construction and demolition sites. Sometimes at the edge of roads you will find construction pipes (the kind that are square, with round holes), which can be used as planters, pedestals, or fixtures for spotlights (put the bulb inside). Many people who can't relate to industrial objects love natural, organic things such as branches, stones, shells, animal skulls, leaves, and dried flowers.

When you look for aesthetic potential in the odd objects in your path, you'll begin to see the world in

169

a new way. It will probably seem more ugly, more beautiful, and especially more vivid. This experience is more important than what you find. The seeing is the key to understanding art.

There are four common faults in presenting art. It's not properly lit; it's poorly placed; it's poorly framed, pedestaled, or whatever; it's not given enough space.

Paintings require a lot of light. So do knick-knacks on shelves. Even free-standing sculpture usually needs more light than it gets. Sculptors put enormous care into selecting splendid materials and then perfecting them. Polished marble, wood, or metal should be shining in a good light, not hidden in a dark corner.

The best way to check if you've adequate light is to take a bright light or spotlight and shine it on the objects you've displayed. This will probably reveal first that the glass in the picture frames is smudged and there's grime in the corners of the china figurines. But after a cleaning, colors and details that have been obscured for years will come to life.

The usual professional approach to lighting art is to supplement general light with individual light for each object: a light over each painting, a light in each shelf, and so forth. If this isn't practical, you can direct light from overhead, from the side, or from below.

There are some art works that are meant to be seen at a distance and some that must be seen from very close. You should know the ideal range for viewing your art and place it accordingly. A painting that is meant to be viewed from ten feet can be hung behind a sofa or table (but not too high). However, you should be able to walk right up to a display of Fabergé Easter eggs. In a foyer, where no one sits down, it makes sense to hang a painting at eye level or slightly above, assuming there's sufficient space for viewing. But in a room where people will most often be sitting, consider hanging a painting lower. It's a very pleasant experience to look directly at a painting while at rest.

If your friends aren't too clumsy, you can probably move some art objects away from the periphery of a space, closer to where people gather. For example, in the home of a publishing executive I built a set of banquettes in a U shape, with a lighted platform in the center for sculpture.

If you have a beautiful painting or sculpture, don't get a frame or pedestal or background drape that competes with it. You can't make a painting any more important by sticking it into a massive, elaborate gilt frame. But you can kill it.

A frame, pedestal, niche, or whatever, used to set off a piece of art, should function only to visually separate the art from the surroundings. It should be simple. Of course a frame shouldn't clash with the art, but it isn't meant to "match" it or decorate it. Often the plainest arrangements of wood, stainless steel, or glass make the best frames. If you have a work by an artist you know, take his or her advice in framing. A good dealer also knows how to show off his pieces to best effect. Use the framer he recommends.

Now and then I still come across decorating experts who advise hanging a cluster of paintings or prints together on a wall. You may see this in muse-

Up light can be directed through a translucent shelf (down light is used as well here). The niche is a natural frame.

171

ums, but usually because there isn't enough money or space for a better setup. The ideal is to put *nothing* near a painting, statue, or any object you want to enjoy for itself. In placing a sculpture or other free-standing object, you have to be careful that the background really stays in the background. In many rooms it's impossible to isolate a sculpture sufficiently, unless it's placed against a wall or in a niche. What's best is an alcove or corner, well lit, and with enough room for walking around the sculpture.

There's no point in having art if you've become so accustomed to it you don't really see it any more. After a few years, it's common to stop perceiving what's in your home, except perhaps when new guests visit and you can see again through their eyes.

The best way to avoid jadedness is to move things around every couple of years or so. The most practical time is when you're painting or buying new lighting or making similar changes. Take the time to reassess your art and accessories. You will have grown more fond of some things and tired of others. You may miss the items put on the third floor and be bored with the ones in the living room. So change them.

I have a couple of boxes of accessories I've just put away for the time being. In a few years it will be like Christmas when I open them up. But there's an even better way of coping with the inevitable accumulation of whatnots: When a friend admires one of them, give it to him.

172

CONCLUSION

To try to be someone you're not is boring. But becoming someone you'd like to be is exciting. Your home is your lifespace—for doing, changing, becoming.

What should your goals be for your home? What should your designer's goals be? When I work, first I try to understand my clients' personalities and what they want in their homes. But what they tell me they want isn't usually what they get, because I take them a lot further than they thought they were going. If I can't extend a client's imagination, he or she doesn't need me.

What kinds of personalities do I meet? I could write a book, and I plan to. But there are a few basic types. Are you authoritative? Organized? Strict with your children? If so, you obviously need a structured environment. But you've probably already built one. What you have to watch out for is becoming too rigid. What you may really need more than anything else is some space that's unformed, free, consciousness-expanding, and completely relaxing. If you're disorganized and easy going, your home is probably already homey, maybe too much so. You may need a structure for keeping order. If you're compulsive, always polishing and neatening, you can live with and appreciate exotic fabrics, crystal, porcelain and the like. Many compulsive people are what I call "nearsighted." They see all the detail around them. They fuss over it and love it. Others are completely different: They want empty space and clean surfaces. The nearsighted person has to be aware of confusion and cuteness. The one who wants wide open spaces may end up with a barren, cold home.

Design to satisfy your basic character, but always include something different, something you wouldn't ordinarily choose, something that makes you react to the world in a new way. If you usually surround yourself with detail, have one room that's simple and quiet. If you tend toward a barren look, include some objects or patterns that are small and delicate. A plain environment is a beautiful background for finely detailed work.

When creating or re-doing your home, consider using a designer. Despite my warnings against The Wallpaper League, a good designer can help you to have the home you want quickly and effectively. Of course, the question is how do you know if your designer is good—and right for you.

As you see his or her work taking shape in your home, you should have a sense of excitement. You should be looking forward to what will be done next. If instead you feel distaste and dread, have the work stopped at once. Call an emergency meeting. Things aren't likely to get better by themselves. A new approach, perhaps a new designer, is needed.

In the end your home should be everything you always dreamed of and more. I'm being almost completely serious. Maybe perfection isn't possible. But it truly is possible to have a home that you love, feel proud of, feel good in. It doesn't have to meet some magazine photographer's or museum curator's ideas of what's sophisticated. Your home is not for them, and it's not for the ages. It's for you and your friends, today and tomorrow. The future will take care of itself. If you feel at home in your home today, your home is all that it should be.